C000131828

Jeff Bezos

Biography of a Billionaire

Business Titan

By
Elliot Reynolds

Table of Contents

Introduction

When Amazon founder and CEO Jeff Bezos opened his company for business, he told his family and friends that it would not last more than a few years. In the mid-1990s, with a growing online world, Bezos felt that his newly created book business would go bankrupt because of notable bookstores such as Barnes & Noble. Today, we know that Bezos was not correct in his assumptions as Amazon has become one of the biggest companies in the world. While Bezos hoped his company would grow, he never imagined that it would turn into the online store that it has.

This book is more than just a biography on Jeff Bezos. It is a biography with a special focus on Bezos' entrepreneurial leadership skills. It is a biography which follows Bezos' personal belief that he can help other people achieve their business career goals in life, just as he did. In this book, you will read about Bezos early life and how his childhood days laid the groundwork for the Jeff Bezos we know today.

I will not just focus on Bezos' main company, Amazon. I will also discuss how he established an educational camp for children as a teenager because he disliked working at McDonalds. I will discuss his philanthropy, how he has kept politics out of his business but also maintains political connections. I will also discuss his other business adventures from Blue Origin to his recent purchase of *The Washington Post*.

In order to make this biography of Bezos one in which follows his own personal beliefs on helping people grow and learn through him, I will discuss various pieces of advice he gives during his presentations. On top of this, the book will look at how Bezos did his best to find a balance between his work and personal life. While he is now recently divorced, Bezos was married for about 25 years to someone who stood by him as a struggling businessman and as one of the most successful businessmen of this generation.

The first chapter is an introduction to the life of the boy who would grow up to run one of the most successful e-commerce businesses of the modern era, Jeff Bezos. While this part of Bezos' life isn't heavily discussed, partly because this biography is meant to bring out the business side of Bezos and partly because he remains a private man, this chapter gives you a sense of the world Bezos saw at an early age. A world which would help mold his business side.

The second chapter looks more in-depth about Bezos as he started to become his own person under the wings of his mother, stepfather, and his maternal grandparents. It discusses how Bezos started working at an early age at his grandfather's ranch, spent his free time reading about science and performing scientific experiments, and got his first job as a teenager working at a fast food restaurant. This chapter also briefly discusses one of Bezos' first entrepreneurial attempts as a teenager, one in which he focused on creating an educational camp for children.

Chapter three briefly focuses on Bezos as he graduated from high school with top honors and went on to college, where he continued to be one of the top students in his class. Even as a student, Bezos showed that he had high intelligence and was academically gifted. This chapter also looks at Bezos' few jobs he held after his years in college.

Chapter four really starts to get into the life of Jeff Bezos the business titan. This chapter focuses on how Bezos built up Amazon from nothing. It discusses his leap of faith when he decided to leave the comforts of his job on Wall Street, move, and start up his own business in Seattle, Washington. From there, the chapter looks into how the top e-commerce retail giant known as Amazon came to be. I will not only look into how the Amazon empire came to be, but I will also discuss the struggles that Bezos faced while he tried to make Amazon into what it is today. In the end, I will look at reasons why people think Amazon continued to grow over other e-commerce stores of the internet's early days.

Chapter five takes a look at one of Jeff Bezos' newest business involvements called Blue Origin. This organization came to be because Bezos has always believed that the future of the world is colonizing space. Therefore, he established his own company which focuses on creating a way to get people, who are not specifically trained as astronauts, into space so humans can start setting up communities where they can live. One of the main reasons Bezos wants to focus on this is because he feels this is one way that we can all protect our earth for the future.

Chapter six looks at a couple of business ventures that Bezos has a hand in, such as Bezos Expeditions and the Washington Post. Similar to Amazon, when Bezos bought The Washington Post a few years ago, he had no idea about the newspaper business. He was never a journalist and never studied journalism. However, when Bezos realized that this newspaper was going under, he knew that he had the strengths needed to keep it going, and he was not wrong. Since buying the business, Bezos has managed to turn The Washington Post around, so that it reached online traffic like it has never seen before.

Chapter seven takes a brief look at Bezos' personal life again as it discusses how he handles both a family and a professional life. This is often a balance that people struggle with, but not Bezos. In fact, he credits the fact that he can manage both a personal and professional life because he doesn't believe in the work and life balance. Instead, he looks at the two as interconnecting to form one. For Bezos, this is a very important piece of information for anyone interested in having a career, especially one where you will often be working trying to keep your company successful. Bezos states that if anyone mentions trying to find a work and life balance during an interview for Amazon, he refuses to hire them.

Chapter eight gives you various tips from Jeff Bezos about starting up your own company. These tips were carefully chosen and are some of Bezos' strongest and most important tips he gives to any entrepreneur. Some of the tips I will discuss for you are ignoring the advice you get from other business owners (yes, Bezos states this includes him), making sure you have faith, how you shouldn't overthink your decisions, and sometimes it's best to go slow and steady.

Chapter nine is one of the biggest chapters of the book as it focuses on the many business lessons that Bezos often shares with people. These are lessons that he discusses learning throughout his career, even as he first started Amazon back in 1995. Altogether, there are countless business lessons which Bezos has discussed over the years. In this book, I discuss over 30 of these lessons, most of which Bezos typically discusses during his interviews and when he is presenting. Some of the business lessons I will touch on in this book are realizing your limits, how you shouldn't be afraid to invent, you shouldn't be afraid to take risks, how you should remember that your marketing strategies can change, and how you should always be willing to do what you tell other people to do.

From Bezos' business lessons, we take a bit of a different turn and focus on how Bezos believes it is important to give back as a business titan in chapter ten. While he typically remains quiet about the charities he gives to, he often gives to charities which follow their missions in science and education. Over the years, many people have called Bezos stingy as a philanthropist, however, this is mainly because most people don't realize all that Bezos does when he gives back to not only his community but also the world. In this chapter, I will discuss Bezos' most public form of philanthropy today, which is his one day fund.

In chapter eleven I will briefly discuss how politics and business go hand in hand for Bezos, even though he does whatever he can to make sure his company has little to do with politics. Unlike many other businesses around today, Bezos has never established a business simply because of politics. However, this doesn't mean that Amazon has not seen its share of politics or that Bezos has not been caught in the middle.

Chapter twelve will look at an important factor for any business person and this is what motivates Jeff Bezos. In this chapter, I will not only discuss why motivation is important for anyone who has a career but also what specific factors tend to motivate one of the biggest CEOs in modern history.

In chapter thirteen, I will take a look at various forms of advice that Bezos is often heard giving his audience and employees. Some of the advice I will discuss is making sure you get enough sleep, not having regrets, keeping your childlike sense of wonder, and being a role model for your competitors. This advice can tie into some of Bezos' business lessons, however, they are separate because Bezos himself states that these things are simply advice he would give anyone, not just someone who is going out into the business world. However, they are also forms of advice that he uses in his daily life, whether at home or at work.

Chapter fourteen will take a brief look into the future of Amazon. Many people often wonder what is going to happen next when it comes to Amazon. While this can often be a bit of a challenge because Bezos likes to keep things private within the Amazon camp, many people have an idea of a few things that Amazon has tried lately and might continue to improve and release in the future.

Chapter 1: Early Life

One of the wealthiest men in the United States goes by the name of Jeff Bezos. Best known as the man who launched Amazon, Bezos was born on January 12, 1964, in Albuquerque, New Mexico as Jeffrey Preston Jorgensen to Ted and Jacklyn (Gise) Jorgensen. At the time of his birth, Bezos' parents struggled like most young couples. Jacklyn, who was only 17 years old, was trying to finish her high school education while Ted worked a minimum wage job. On top of this, Ted was a struggling alcoholic. Jacklyn officially left her husband when Bezos was about a year and a half. She then worked while she tried to raise her son as a single mom.

From an early age, Bezos started showing signs that he was intelligent. He would often do things that most kids his age would not be able to do. For example, he wanted to start sleeping in a bigger bed, so as a toddler he took a screwdriver and took apart his crib. He figured that if his crib was brought down that he would be able to obtain a bigger bed. At the same time, Jacklyn started dating a Cuban immigrant known as Miguel Bezos, usually referred to as Mike.

When Bezos was around four years old, his mother remarried making Mike Bezos' stepfather. Mike then adopted Bezos, which is when his name changed from Jorgensen to Bezos. At the time, Mike was attending college at the University of New

Mexico. After he obtained his degree, Mike received a position as an engineer for Exxon in Houston, Texas. Therefore, the family moved and Bezos began attending Oaks Elementary School in the fourth grade. By this time, Bezos was an older brother to a sister named Christina and a brother named Mark.

Throughout his childhood, Bezos focused on becoming the best person he could be. He was raised Catholic and never had any trouble learning. However, he would often become bored in the classroom. Therefore, Bezos was sent to a gifted program at his school. This program would be able to challenge Bezos in ways that the typical classroom could not. He would be able to learn not only the regular course studies, but also be able to focus on other things, such as scientific experiments.

Bezos learned around the age of 10 that Mike was not his biological father but had adopted him as a young child. This makes Bezos one of the many successful businessmen who were adopted, such as Steve Jobs. Some people feel that one of the reasons Bezos strived to become successful in his childhood and early adult years was because he wanted to prove himself to his biological father. He wanted to show him that he could make something of himself. However, many other people feel that the reason Bezos has become so successful is not only because of his high intelligence but his determination, business strategies, and his personality, which will be discussed later in this book.

Whether he went to school in New Mexico or Florida, Bezos teachers quickly learned of his high intelligence. In fact, when interviewed, one teacher stated that she believed there were no limits to what Bezos was capable of. However, she also stated that he would need to have a little guidance in order to reach his full potential.

Before he entered high school, Bezos was reading at a high school level. In fact, he read so much that he was able to obtain a special reader's certificate. On top of this, teachers allowed him to join in on knowledge bowl type competitions which were reserved for juniors and seniors in high school. He entered a few competitions where he had to present different scientific projects. By this point, many people in the community were learning about the gifted child in the 6th-grade classroom. However, Bezos never seemed to let his high intelligence get the best of him. Instead, he just focused on doing what he loved to do, which was to learn and invent.

Even though Bezos was known as one of the gifted kids in his school, he remained popular. He was always willing to help other students learn and wasn't afraid to challenge authority. If he knew that something wasn't right, he wasn't afraid to let anyone know. He felt that in order to truly learn, people needed to ask questions and learn the truth. Even though many people felt that Bezos didn't demonstrate good leadership skills, he was still known to do what he could to help those around him. As a child, Bezos started to practice the traits that would lead him to become one of the most successful businessmen of his generation. Everything he did as a child planted the seeds for his adulthood. However, all this might not have been possible without the love and support from his family and friends around him.

Bezos' early life was filled with people who supported his interests and pushed him to receive the best education possible, inside and outside of school. Bezos first started to become interested in entrepreneurship as a child. During the summers, he would go visit his mother's parents at their Cotulla, Texas ranch. It was also during this time that Bezos started to show an interest in technology and science. He was also able to travel with them around the United States and Canada as his grandparents were members of a Caravan Club. This is a club where people who enjoy traveling get together in specified locations, usually designated for club members. Here, they can enjoy the benefits of RV type living without having to figure out all the details of their travel arrangements themselves. On top of that, club members feel this is a safe way to travel as they don't have to worry about what type of area they are traveling to.

He would often find various things to invent, such as an

electric arm which became useful for when he wanted to keep his younger brothers and sisters out of his room. Other inventions that Bezos tried as a child were a solar cooker made out of tin foil and an umbrella, which didn't work too well, and an automatic gate closer, which he made out of tires filled with cement.

However, Bezos didn't stop with just his inventions. He also wanted the best for those around him, especially his family. For example, Bezos wanted his grandmother to stop smoking. He tried to get her to quit her habit by using emotions but when this didn't work, he decided to turn to mathematics. He asked her a series of questions, such as when she started smoking and how many cigarettes she smokes a day. He then told his grandmother that since she started smoking, she had taken about nine years off of her life. Fortunately, this information was enough to make Bezos' grandmother stop smoking.

Chapter 2: A Growing Entrepreneur

Bezos' interest in science and engineering started when he was a child. He would often be found in his parents' garage where he would be inventing something that could be used around the house or working on scientific experiments. However, Bezos' experiments didn't stop at his parents' house. He would also spend some of his time working on inventions and scientific experiments when he stayed with his grandparents. Bezos started working as a young child at his grandfather's ranch, where he would mainly castrate cattle and repair windmills. He would stay there during the summer, starting at around the age of 5 until he was about 16 years old. Later in his life, Bezos would talk about how it was his grandfather Gise who became a huge inspiration to him. One of the quotes that impacted Bezos the most was when his grandfather stated, "...it's harder to be kind than clever." To Bezos, this is one of the many pieces of his life that set him on the road to becoming an entrepreneur.

Bezos' parents, grandparents, and friends knew they had a special child, one who not only showed high intelligence but also looked into the future. When he created an invention, he thought about how it would help his family or himself long-term. However, they were not the only ones who knew Bezos was a special child. Many others felt the same way as he was featured in the book, *Turning on bright minds: A parent looks at gifted education in Texas* by Julie Ray. In the book, Ray discusses how a boy named "Tim," who is really Bezos, is a sixth grader in his school's gifted child education program. Not only did he read books well above his grade level, but he also created a survey for all the students to complete in order to rate how well the school's teachers were doing. On top of this, Ray discusses how he was always working on several science experiments and really showed a genuine interest in learning and creating. Furthermore, Ray states that while the boy was usually pretty serious, he also didn't show the greatest leadership skills.[1]

As a child, Bezos was not incredibly athletic but that didn't mean that he couldn't be part of a sports team it just meant he had a different role. Around the time he was in upper elementary school, Bezos decided to join the youth Pee Wee football team. While Bezos was a lot smaller than most of the boys on the team, this didn't matter in the end as he was made captain within a couple of weeks because of his ability to remember every play.

---

[1] "Amazon.com: Customer reviews: Turning on bright minds: A parent looks at gifted education in Texas", 2013.

Whether Bezos knew he was gifted at a young age is debatable. However, what we do know is that Bezos was not shy when it came to telling people, including his teachers, what he thought. As a child, he would often tell people that he was going to become a space entrepreneur. He would tell them "the future of mankind is not on this planet" which made many people believe he would become an astronaut.[2]

It wasn't until the Bezos' moved to Miami, Florida when young Bezos started to get into computers. However, instead of just using computers for what they were developed for, Bezos wanted to dig deeper. He wanted to learn how computers worked and why. He wanted to know how all the pieces inside of the computer worked together in order to create a functioning machine. He also wanted to know everything computers could do. Unlike many people, Bezos believed that computers would be able to do more than what most people ever imagined.

As a teenager, Bezos got his first real job working at McDonald's. He mainly worked in the early hours before he went off to school as a breakfast short order cook.

The Dream Institute

---

[2] Carlson, 2011.

It was throughout his early years that he knew he did not really want to work a typical job. He knew he wanted to do something different. This realization became even more important as a teenager. While he worked at McDonald's, Bezos and his girlfriend decided that they wanted to start up a summer camp. They called the camp "The Dream Institute" with the vision of creating an educational place where fourth through sixth graders could go to learn. The price for a child to go to this camp was $600 and the campers would stay there for about ten days. The first year, Bezos received six signups and created a reading lesson plan for the campers. The list of books which Bezos included gives an inside look into the young child's brain.

In total, there were at least eleven books and plays which were included in the lesson plan.

1. Stranger in a Strange Land by Robert A. Heinlein.

2. The Once and Future King by T.H. White

3. The Lord of the Rings by J.R.R. Tolkien

4. *Dune* by Frank Herbert

5. *Our Town* by Thornton Wilder

6. *Watership Down* by Richard Adams

7. Gulliver's Travels by Jonathan Swift

8. *Black Beauty* by Anna Sewell

9. *The Matchmaker* by Thornton Wilder

10. *David Copperfield* by Charles Dickens

11. *Treasure Island* by Robert Louis Stevenson

Chapter 3: Bezos Enters into the Adult World

From High School to College

As Bezos continued high school his interest in science continued to grow. He was one of the students that went to a Student Science Training Program on the University of Florida's campus. Bezos graduated from high school in 1982 as valedictorian. On top of this, Bezos was not only a Silver Knight Award winner but also a National Merit Scholar. In his valedictorian speech, Bezos talked about space and how it should be colonized. For most people, Bezos' speech was not surprising as he had spent his childhood talking about how the future of Earth was out in space.

After receiving early admission, Bezos attended Princeton University where he majored in computer science and electrical engineering. Throughout his undergraduate years, Bezos was a member of Phi Beta Kappa. On top of this, he was elected to Tau Beta Pi, an honorary engineering program, and became President of the Students for the Exploration and Development of Space for the program's Princeton chapter. He graduated from Princeton in 1986 with a 4.2 GPA and his Bachelors of Science degree.

Later in his life, Bezos stated that one of the biggest things he learned at Princeton was that he was not smart enough to become a physicist, which is why he switched his major to computer science. However, people are not completely sure that this was the real reason as before he went into college he told the Miami Herald that he was going to focus on computers as they had been an interest of his since the fourth grade. The things Bezos learned in his computer classes surprised him.

As he entered his classes, he felt that he was going to be taught how to hack into computers. Instead, he was taught about algorithms and how to develop software. This brought more about what computers can do for people to Bezos' mind than he had ever imagined. While Bezos did not know about it at the time, this would be another stepping stone for his future career.

Bezos couldn't wait to jump into the computer world. In fact, he didn't want to wait until after college, so he went home one summer and started to show his parents what he learned about computers at Princeton. He showed his stepfather what computers were really capable of doing and what algorithms are and how to go about creating your own algorithm. After seeing what his son showed him, Mike went back to his company and realized that what Bezos had learned could be useful. So, while the family was spending the summer in Norway while Mike was on business with Exxon, Bezos received a job as a programmer for the company over the summer. He couldn't have been more excited. While he was not perfect at the job, as he was just learning himself, he spent time doing what he loved, making money, and continuing to learn about computer programming. With every mistake he learned, Bezos took each one as a learning experience and never made the same mistake twice.

However, Bezos would not jump on the career path he chose for himself in college immediately. In fact, after graduation, he wanted a different adventure. Therefore, he traveled to Wall Street and fell in love with the competitive culture of that area. Bezos had always had a competitive nature about him. Even throughout his elementary and high school years. He prided himself on the fact that he would outperform people who were years older than him. This personality characteristic stayed with Bezos as he entered New York City.

From College to Professional Careers

When he graduated from Princeton in 1987, he showed everyone under his picture in Princeton's yearbook that he wasn't going to let anyone tell him no when it came to what he wanted to do with his life. By this time, Bezos had made up his mind. He not only wanted to work with technology, especially computers, but he also wanted to invent new technology and he wanted to be the CEO of his own company.

However, he also knew that he would need additional job experience before he could take on his own company.

One of the biggest reasons Bezos felt he needed to gain more experience was because he had no idea what an entrepreneur would do. Another reason was he had no idea what type of company he wanted to start. Even though Bezos always tells young entrepreneurs today that they need to pick whatever they are passionate about, Bezos didn't have his own advice at the time. He wasn't sure if he needed to pick something that would for sure make him money or a company that was different from all the rest. There was still a lot of investigating that Bezos had to do in order to reach his decision.

Therefore, Bezos acted on his knowledge that when finding a job right out of college, he had to find one that would teach him about being an entrepreneur. He figured that while he was learning this new career path, he would be able to figure out what type of store he wanted to open over time.

Bezos did not have a difficult time landing a job in his field of interest. He had held nearly perfect grades in college and had always shown potential in his chosen career. Among the many companies which tried to hire Bezos were Bell Labs, Intel, and Fitel. Ultimately, it was Fitel that Bezos decided to work for. He chose this company because he knew that Fitel would be the best fit for him in his endeavor to learn some entrepreneurial skills. The company was young and there was room for Bezos to not only learn but to grow. In a sense, this was the first leap of faith that Bezos often discusses in his speeches and interviews today. This was the first real time that he took a chance on something where he wasn't sure how it would fully turn out. While he had done this in other areas of his life before, this time it was different. Bezos was now on his own and he was working towards something he really wanted to do. While it was a bit scary, he knew that there was not a better job out there for him. At the same time, he found the position to be challenging and risky, which was a major draw for Bezos.

A Job Which Brings the Love of the Internet to Bezos

The founders of the Fitel Company, Geoffrey Heal and Graciela Chichilnisky, were two professors from Columbia University's Department of Economics. When asked about why they started the company, the pair stated it was something like a small internet before the internet became popular. In the main building of Fitel, which is known as Equinet, different computers were linked together from different investment and brokerage firms. Using this method, the company had set up a way for people to buy and sell trades between themselves, similar to how people see the online stock market today.

One of the main reasons Bezos received this job was because he was skilled at the computer, something other employees were not and, even if they were, they never came close to knowing the things that Bezos could accomplish. However, most people who worked with Bezos, whether on his side or the other side of the computer, believed he was an investment banker.

Years later, the founders would tell reporters that there was no way their company would be anything like what it is today without Bezos. Chichilnisky has stated that she would design the system and then let Bezos build it. Because of his knowledge with computers, he built it beyond anything they ever imagined. If he made a mistake, he was able to go back and fix the system so it ran better than ever. However, there was hardly ever a time when Bezos needed to fix anything with the system. Since this was a newer system, something that other companies were not doing, the founders thought that the system would have its problems and they expected this to happen often. To their surprise, problems rarely happened.

Instead, the biggest challenge for the company was to get people to believe that their system worked. Most people said no to the system until they found a company called Salomon Brothers, who allowed Fitel to set up the system in their office. Even though they could see the system and knew how it worked, the owner continued to believe it was some type of trick.

Because Bezos excelled in his career, he was able to quickly work his way up to become the Head of Development. From there, he went on to become the Director of Customer Service and eventually became the second in command. By this time, Bezos was in his early 20s and managing almost two dozen computer programs among the company's offices. While the company believed they had found a golden employee with Bezos, he kept dreaming about his secret entrepreneurial path. He hadn't told anyone in the company that this is what he officially wanted to do with his life. And while he was learning more about running a business, he also felt that there were other avenues for him when it came to learning how to be an entrepreneur.

Bezos worked for Fitel for a couple of years. Later in his life, he stated that he didn't agree with the way they ran the business. The company had just started a few years before and had Bezos traveling from New York to London every week. Bezos didn't believe that this was the right way to start-up a company. This type of traveling costs a lot of money, which is something that start-up companies don't generally have. Bezos felt that the company could become bankrupt in the near future.

However, this doesn't mean that Bezos didn't learn from the

company, in fact, Fitel put him on the path to setting up his interest in the internet. While no one knew that the internet was going to come in the near future, Bezos knew that the programs he built at Fitel and the way people could trade stocks were going to be a part of the world's future. It was only a matter of time. What he didn't realize was that the future internet would play such an important role in his entrepreneurial dream.

Bezos Continues Working towards His Entrepreneurial Dream

In 1988, Bezos decided to take a different direction in his career as he started working for Bankers Trust. Like Fitel, he found this company to be working towards computers as they were trying to find ways that computers could be used to help the banking world. He first received a job there as assistant vice president, where he helped them build the computers they wanted in order to make their jobs easier. Because of Bezos' intelligence with computer programming, he quickly received a position as the manager.

While at Bankers Trust, Bezos ran an engineering department and created a network known as BTWorld, which allowed communications via the computer. Because of Bezos' work at Fitel, he was quickly able to design and build what the company wanted. However, he was also able to take the company a bit farther than they imagined as the computer program became a part of over 100 large corporations. Because of this, these businesses could communicate closely with Bankers Trust through the computer program. Of course, for Bezos, developing the program was easy. It was getting people to believe that the program worked which was the challenge. But, this was a challenge that Bezos was slowly becoming used to. In fact, he had started to incorporate different ways to get people to believe that what he had done would work and work well. People were hardly ever disappointed and if something did go wrong with the system, Bezos was able to fix it quickly. However, people rarely saw any type of problem.

On the side of Bankers Trust, they couldn't believe that the program allowed them to track the performance of things such as investing, profit-sharing, and pension funds. Because of this, the company was able to replace their paper reports which they used to send off to clients. Instead, they could send these reports electronically, which was a feat that amazed their clients. Of course, there were always a number of clients that wanted to continue to receive their paper trail and this included many employees of the bank. When looking back on working with Bezos, the president of Bankers Trust at that time, Harvey Hirsch, stated that Bezos just saw things differently than everyone else did. He could see what the future of the world was and he truly believed that computers were it. On top of that, he knew that the system he had built would become bigger and better and spread out into the world. While most people doubted Bezos, he knew he was right – and he was.

Over time, everyone came to enjoy the new electronic way that Bankers Trust could communicate with them and this change of heart often came because of Bezos himself. Ever since his childhood days, Bezos had a way of persuasion that could cause almost anyone to believe what he believed. As he grew, he learned that one of the best ways to get people to believe what he did was simply by stating it as fact and having authority in his statements. On top of this, Bezos never had any trouble with telling people that he was right and they were wrong. For many people of Bankers Trust, especially the president of the company, what was more amazing was not his persuasion but how professional he could be while he told people they weren't thinking in the right direction. He could do this in a way that hardly ever irritated someone or made them angry, which is always a difficult thing to do when you are telling people that they are wrong. As Hirsch believed, this was just another one of Bezos' many hidden talents that would lead him into the Amazon world.

However, it would only take Bezos a couple of years working at Bankers Trust to become a little bored. He no longer felt that his position was challenging and he still felt that he had a lot to learn before he could start his own company. Therefore, he decided to send out his resume to a select group of companies. Bezos began working for D.E. Shaw & Company, another newly established hedge fund company, and Bezos wasted no time learning as much he could about the company and helping them grow. Bezos loved the fact that the company was established in 1988 as he felt with the company only being a few years old, he would be able to learn as much as he could about being an entrepreneur.

In order to do this, he became close with the company's founder, David Shaw. He had come up with the idea to found the company because he wanted to create a computer automated trading system that investors could use on Wall Street. Bezos started to look up to Shaw because he believed that the way Shaw had started his company was similar to what Bezos was trying to do.

Bezos also liked this job because the software program was already developed. He could learn a new system after development, which gave Bezos a different look into the world of computer software. Because of Bezos' background and natural talent with computer programming, he was able to work his way up to become D.E. Shaw's fourth president by the time he was 30 years old. While many felt this was young for the type of position Bezos held, he still had his dream of starting up his own business and began to feel that he was getting too old and needed to act sooner rather than later. Therefore, he started to wonder what the best course of action would be.

Some people believe that if it wasn't for David Shaw, Bezos would have never taken the leap to start up Amazon. However, Bezos looked up to Shaw and believed that Shaw himself had taken this leap with his own company. As Bezos looked around and saw how well D.E. Shaw was doing, he started to wonder if it really was time for himself to start his own entrepreneurial dream. After all, he felt he had learned a lot over the years, especially from Shaw who he believed was a great entrepreneur and had a natural talent for it, like many people believe Bezos has today.

The Internet Sparks the Mind of Bezos

After Bezos had been working with David Shaw for a about a year and a half, Shaw asked him to look into a new thing that was making waves in the news – the internet. Bezos himself had heard a bit about this program and had started to wonder what it was. Therefore, Bezos jumped on the opportunity. Like Shaw, Bezos felt that the internet was going to create new avenues for businesses, especially ones such as D.E. Shaw. After all, Bezos had already developed programs which allowed investors to trade remotely.

This wasn't the first time Bezos heard of the internet. It had actually been around a bit longer than what the public really knew. However, it was mainly used on college campuses and in the government as a way for governmental agencies to connect with each other. Through the internet, they started to exchange information which was very different than trading stocks.

A Very Brief History of the Internet

While most people did not know this at the time, the internet had been around since before the 1990s. However, it was in 1989 when a man named Tim Berners-Lee created the World Wide Web, the first internet browser. It would be two years later, in 1991, when the World Wide Web became available for commercial use. Of course, many companies were cautious of the internet at first and it took a couple of years for it to really kick off. However, once one company started using it, then another company would quickly catch on. When this happened, it didn't take long for the internet to start spreading, specifically in governmental agencies.

On top of this, people kept making changes to the internet in order to better the connection between companies. For example, the University of Illinois developed their own internet, which they called Mosaic. From there, Silicon Valley decided to take matters into their own hands and created a similar product and a company called Netscape came out with a browser known as Navigator.

As Shaw watched one company take the idea and develop a new browser, he started to realize that there was something about the internet that was going to bring everyone into the future. Of course, Bezos had the same thought. However, Bezos never imagined that he would find the growth of the internet to be so large.

As Bezos started researching, he quickly realized that the internet was growing at a rate of over 2,000% annually. This astounded Bezos and he soon found himself trying to find out everything he could about this new program. As Bezos said later in his life during an interview about his D.E. Shaw days, "You know things just don't grow that fast. It's highly unusual, and that started me thinking, 'What kind of business plan might make sense in the context of that growth?'"[3] Because Bezos understands business, he knew that this type of growth is incredibly impressive. In fact, it's a type of growth that you do not often see. Basically, it meant that the population growth for the internet grew annually by a factor of 23. This means that if you are at a store with 100 people and the population of this store grows at 2,300% in one year, the population would then be 2,400 customers. Because the starting point of the internet was very low, this made the

---

[3] Brandt, 2011.

percentage in 1993-1994 even more impressive in Bezos' mind.

Bezos also quickly realized that this is exactly what he was looking for. While he didn't know much about the World Wide Web, he was learning and the more he learned the more he knew he needed a piece of the internet. In fact, when Bezos thinks back to this time in his life today, he states that he is still amazed by the growth he saw when he did his research on the internet. He stated that there weren't a lot of people he knew of in this world that had seen such growth. Another thing that amazed him, mostly because of how fast the internet was growing yearly, was how many people were still overly cautious about it. While Bezos wanted to jump right in when it came to the internet, most people he knew weren't sure they wanted anything to do with it.

Both Shaw and Bezos had the same idea that when something grew that fast, it meant that it created a lot of opportunities. For Bezos, this was one of the last pieces of strength he needed in order to officially make his leap into starting his own company. While he still wasn't sure what type of company he would start, he did know that it was going to be a part of the World Wide Web. Unlike other people Bezos had worked for, Shaw knew that he needed to go places beyond D.E. Shaw. While he didn't like seeing Bezos leave the company, he also knew that whatever Bezos decided to do, he was going to do it well and go far with his company. However, no one, including Shaw, could predict just how far Bezos was going to go with a company he would start about a year later.

Bezos' four years in high school were only a minor stepping stone into the entrepreneurial giant he would later become. While he received a lot of support for being one of the smartest students in the school, no one knew that he would one day become one of the richest men in the world. In fact, during his high school years, Bezos knew that he wanted to manage his own company but he thought it would be something to do with science or space. While he would eventually come to found a space exploration company with his own thoughts about colonizing space with humans, this isn't what he is known for today and not the company that made him one of the richest men. Furthermore, his space company, which is known as Blue Origin, is not even the company that taught Bezos most about customer service and running a business.

Chapter 4: Amazon

Before I get into how Bezos founded Amazon, I want to take time to discuss how Bezos came to his business decision of opening a bookstore that was going to blossom into Amazon. As Bezos came to recognize at D.E. Shaw, there was one main thing entrepreneurs did when deciding to develop their company and that was they went into something they were passionate about. While Bezos understood this, he felt he still had a problem. He wasn't really passionate about anything other than the growth of the internet. Bezos was passionate about becoming a part of that growth. He wanted his company to become a part of that growth.

As Bezos thought about the best type of store for him, he came to think about books. While there were a lot of major bookstores across the country, such as Barnes and Noble, Bezos knew that with his knowledge of computer programming and his recent knowledge with the internet, he could create something that not even Barnes and Noble had – a bookstore completely on the internet.

In all honesty, no one but Bezos really knows why he decided to pick books. While he does love books, he isn't really passionate about books. However, it was a company that he knew he could figure out and grow into something better from there. Whether, at this moment, Bezos thought of increasing the products in his bookstore is unknown. However, it wouldn't take long for Bezos to jump on the bandwagon of continually adding products and services. In fact, starting from the time Bezos decided to leave D.E. Shaw and start his own company, he never stopped believing in the leap of faith he took.

Books and the Flow List

Of course, Bezos put a lot of thought into realizing that he wanted to create a bookstore. Later in his life, Bezos would state, "I was looking for something that you could only do online, something that couldn't be replicated in the physical world."[4] Throughout his thought process, Bezos created what he called a flow list, which is one of the many steps that helped the young entrepreneur realize that he will, eventually, sell more than books in his business. This list consisted of:

Competition

While Bezos doesn't focus too much on the competition now, and Amazon never really has, he also knew that while making his decision to sell books there were at least two popular bookstores in the country, Barnes and Noble and the Border's Group. He also learned that when they were combined

---

[4] Brandt, 2011.

together, they had a market share of 25%.

While looking into how customers could order books, he found it was possible but it wasn't the easiest process. Fortunately, for Bezos at the time, neither one of these stores had started using the internet as a way to sell books. Therefore, customers still had to go into a branch store or call the store to see if they could purchase a specific book. However, this didn't mean that the book chain would be able to come across the book the customer was requesting.

When Bezos learned about this, he decided that the internet would be the perfect opportunity to fix this problem. However, he also had to find a way to try to get the books people wanted that Barnes and Noble or the Border's Group couldn't get for their customers. On top of this, Bezos learned that he also needed to expand his bookstore as all the other bookstores he looked into had a limited selection. He knew that this would be helpful through the internet. At this point, one of his biggest concerns became how he would get an inventory going. However, Bezos always knew there was a way and even if he had to wait to purchase the book until a customer bought it themselves, he was going to make sure the customer received the book.

As the internet kept growing, so did Bezos' competition, before he even looked into starting his own bookstore, or even did research on the internet, a couple of newly formed bookstores, such as Computer Literacy Bookstore, started their own online company. So, it wasn't that there were no bookstores on the internet, but Bezos found these stores to have fewer items available in stock, which became a selling point for him. Plus, Bezos knew that with his experience with developing programs and computers, along with everything he was learning about the World Wide Web, he could easily create a better online system for selling books.

Shipping Costs

Shipping costs are still something that Bezos is continually trying to improve. From the beginning, Bezos knew that people would not want to pay for overly expensive shipping costs, therefore, he knew that he needed to start his business off with something that wouldn't affect shipping costs too much. While books are heavier than CDs, they were still easy to ship and fairly inexpensive. At the same time, you could package them well to make sure the item was delivered to the customer in the best condition, which is something Bezos found a little harder to do with CDs.

Other products that Bezos played around with as he was looking into shipping costs were software and electronics. These items were starting to increase rapidly, however, they also carried more worry and money when shipping. At the same time, this did not mean that Bezos would never start to sell CDs, software, or electronics. In fact, this is around the time he started to think that he could include expanding his business into a later part of his business plan, which is something that always remained on Bezos' mind.

How to Acquire Inventory

At first, Bezos was worried this would be one of his main problems, however, he soon found that this wouldn't be a problem at all. In fact, two of the main distributors of the book market, Baker & Taylor and Ingram Book Group had already taken advantage of the digital age. This made everything a bit easier for Bezos as he could simply contact one of these companies and order the books, which would be shipped to him within a couple of days. Then, he could ship it to his customer.

Bezos noted the way the book companies strategically placed their warehouses across the United States. He took note that they had built small warehouses and each warehouse held so many items of each of their books. Because of this system, the company could ship the book from the warehouse closest to you, which meant it would reach the customer within a couple of days. Today, this is how Amazon runs their warehouses. While there is a main headquarters location for Amazon in Seattle, Washington, the company has tons of warehouses scattered throughout the world in order to make sure that their two day or overnight shipping can be fulfilled.

Furthermore, the two companies held about a total of 400,000 books. This was an amazing number for Bezos, who wanted to develop the world's largest online bookstore.

Large Market Size

While Bezos searched for the right item to sell, he was going back and forth between whether he should get into the business of selling music and software or just books. One way Bezos came upon the idea to sell books was because of the large market size of books. For example, Bezos noted that millions of more books were sold than software and CDs. For Bezos, this made books a more viable market, at least at that time. People were just spending more money on books than they were on music.

Familiar Product

Bezos also knew that, above all, he wanted to sell a product that nearly everyone was familiar with. During the early 1990s, while CDs were starting to become popular, many people still wanted regular cassette tapes or just liked to listen to the radio. However, when it came to books, everyone knew about books and everyone had books in their household, whether they were an avid reader or not, people wanted books. Not only did people buy books for themselves, but they considered it a great gift for other people.

On top of this, people felt more comfortable with buying books online. They didn't have to worry about if the book would be a cheap knockoff like they had concerns about when it came to software. Furthermore, they didn't have to worry about anything breaking, which many people did when it came to the shipping of CDs.

Giving Customers Discounts

Bezos knew well that people loved to save money whenever they could. He knew that if people saw the word "sale" they were more likely to buy that product, whether they needed it or not. Therefore, Bezos also wanted to pick something in the market where he could easily create his own discount. After looking into this, Bezos realized that by selling books online, he is already able to give customers a deal whenever he wanted.

A discount bookstore called Crown Books opened in the early 1990s. When this happened, the books this store sold were cheaper than books at other stores. Therefore, many other bookstores had to lower the price of their books in order to keep up with the new competition. Unfortunately, for many of the stores, they ended up going out of business because they couldn't keep up with their lease agreements or rent for their store and keep the prices low at the same time. Because Bezos was selling books online, he wouldn't have to worry about a lot of these costs.

Online Potential

Because Bezos was going to sell his books online, he would have the advantage of being able to use software programs. These programs would allow his customers to search for a book by title, category, or author. Of course, Bezos would establish other searchable categories over time. For example, once he learned that each book had its own ISBN, he decided he could use this number in order to help the customers search for the exact book he or she wanted. At the same time, Bezos understood more about computer software than many other people who were looking at selling books online or even bookstores that hadn't reached the online market yet. He knew that while most stores only had over 100,000 titles in their inventory, computer software could hold millions of titles within its database. This gave Bezos an advantage over other bookstores.

After Bezos completed analyzing his flow list, he realized that starting with books would be his best option. After all, people all over the world bought millions more books than CDs and software combined. On top of this, they were more durable and easy to mail.

As Bezos continued to think about the best way to start his business, he knew at least two things. First, he needed to get a better idea of how to sell books. Second, he needed to look into a better business plan which not only looked at his business in the short-term but also over the long-term. When it came to long-term, Bezos had to look at factors such as where he was going to station his business, who he was going to work with, and if there was anything else he was missing.

Throughout this time, Bezos knew that some things he would learn as he went about starting his business. However, he also knew that he always had to make sure he did his research and as much of it as he possibly could. After all, he didn't want to make such a huge mistake that he would have to close his doors right after he gets his business up and running. For Bezos, the next step was finding out as much as he could learn about selling books.

An Idea Blossoms

Almost a year before Bezos decided to officially launch Amazon, he realized that he had to learn not only about the retail industry but, more importantly, something on how to sell books. Therefore, Bezos looked for an avenue that could help teach him and found out that the American Booksellers Association held classes focused on how to manage your own bookstore. Bezos quickly signed up as he knew this was the best opportunity for him. Little did Bezos know, this class would teach him more than just how to manage his new idea.

The class was a four-day course held in Portland. Bezos had signed up with about fifty other people from young entrepreneurs like himself to retired seniors who were thinking about a second career. Not only did the instructor, Richard Howorth, focus on the financial aspects of a bookstore and how to handle inventory, but he also discussed customer service. Because Howorth was a believer in strict customer service, he spoke a lot about this topic and Bezos listened to every word.

In order to drive the point to his class on how going above and beyond for the customer can change the mood, Howorth, who ran a book store in New York, told a story where he was informed a customer had a complaint. He went to meet the customer, a lady who was extremely angry, and told Howorth that some of the store's dirt from their potted plants had fallen on her car while she was parked in front of the store. Howorth stated that at this point, he could have easily just apologized and let the woman leave angry. However, this was not his policy. Instead, he was going to do what all employees were supposed to do, so he did whatever he could to change her mood. Howorth offered to wash the customer's car.

They drove to the nearest car wash but found it closed. Of course, this only irritated the customer further so Howorth came up with the idea to drive to his house and he would personally wash her car for her. At his house, he grabbed all the supplies he needed and washed her car. As he washed, he began to notice the customer's mood change. Once she drove him back to the store, the customer was no longer angry and couldn't wait to come back again and see what new books the store had on their shelves.

For Bezos, this story was amazing. He had never heard of such perfect customer service. At the end of the class, Bezos went up to Howorth and told him that he was going to do everything he could to give the best customer service possible with his online bookstore. He talked about how that story had inspired him to make sure he goes above and beyond for his customers.

And this is exactly what Bezos did. By 1999, he had hired about 500 customer service employees. Their job was to simply watch the customer comments, go through every single email, answer the phones, and if a customer had a complaint to do whatever they could to fix it. Amazon's policy has never been to try to fix the customer's complaint. It has always been to do what you can to make sure the customer is happy.

Today, Howorth's book store is in direct competition with Amazon and many people had previously spoken to Howorth about how his customer service story influenced the man who is considered one of the richest men in the world due to Amazon. Howorth states that the customer service you give someone face to face is much different than the customer service that Bezos gives his customers. Howorth says when it comes to personal interaction, customer service is more action and emotion whereas online you send an unemotional message apologizing to the customer. Howorth also states that he is very sure Bezos has never washed another person's car.

More than likely, Howorth is right. There is a difference between face to face human interaction with in-person customer service and the type of customer service Bezos and his team give online. Even former employees state there is a big difference. However, they also state that the customer service team still goes above and beyond when they need to deal with a customer complaint. They also state that if they don't and the customer contacts Bezos, the Amazon CEO contacts his employee to see what the story is and try to help the employee in finding ways to better serve Amazon's customers.

At times, Bezos has learned about customer service by making mistakes. For example, during Amazon's early days, the team decided the best policy was to empty a customer's cart if it had been idle for over a month. Unfortunately, there were customers who had spent hours looking for various books to place in their cart and buy over time. Then, one day, the customer would look at their cart and find it empty. After the first email Bezos received from an angry customer who stated he had spent a long time finding just the right books and keeping them in his cart to purchase later and now his cart was empty, Bezos told his team to find a new policy. Then, Bezos met with other members of his team to discuss ways that customers could save items without having to place them in their cart.

The Beginnings of an Empire

The main reason Bezos decided to leave his position at D.E. Shaw was that he knew it was time to go into business for himself. Since he was younger, Bezos had always been interested in developing his own work and now, as an adult, this dream only increased. However, before Bezos officially launched his online book business, he needed money and to perform tests. Most of the money came from his parents, who invested about $100,000. Bezos performed the first sale test on April 3, 1995. But before he could really get started on his business, Bezos needed to find a team which would work with him.

A Couple of Friends, an Accountant, and the Launch of a Company

"There are two kinds of companies. Those that work to try to charge more and those that work to charge less. We will be the second."[5]

Before Bezos even looked for people to work for him, he knew that he wanted to do one thing and that was to create an online bookstore that focused more on the customers than anything else. It was a tactic he had learned through his class and one which he told his teacher that he was going to hold in high regard as he started his own business. From that moment, Bezos made a promise to himself that he would never steer away from what was more important - the customer. To date, this is a promise that Bezos has kept not only for himself but for Amazon and the company's growing customer base.

After Bezos had an idea of his business plan, knew what he wanted to sell and a clear direction for customer service, he only had one last thing to figure out and this was where to go to hire people. Immediately, Bezos knew that he had to create some type of hiring bar as he had to make sure he hired the right people for the company. Even if one of his friends wanted or needed a job, this didn't mean he could get one working for Bezos as he might not be the right person. Therefore, Bezos looked beyond the group of people he knew when trying to find the right couple of people to help lead his

---

[5] Tsagklis, 2018.

company onto the right path.

Remember, when Bezos started Amazon, the internet was available but it was nothing like what we have today. They didn't have social networks like Facebook and they didn't have more professional networks like LinkedIn. Instead, Bezos had to find business partners another way, he had to go back through all of his business connections and see who would be a good fit. On top of this, Bezos knew that he had one more factor stacked against him when looking for someone. His business had hardly any money. This meant that he could not process a check for an employee like most businesses could. Furthermore, Bezos definitely could not pay anyone what other companies could. It would be a factor he would have to strategize carefully to overcome, which is exactly what he did.

Of course, the first place Bezos thought of was D.E. Shaw, however, he could not directly hire someone from that business. Instead, Bezos realized he could contact the people he knew who still worked there and see if they knew of anyone who would be willing to work for him. Therefore, Bezos contacted Peter Laventhol, who had a connection with other engineers. Bezos knew he would need an engineer on his team and he had a lot of trust and respect for Laventhol. Therefore, he knew that whoever Laventhol directed him to, the connection would probably be a good choice.

The first name Laventhol mentioned to Bezos was one of his classmates from his graduate school days at Stanford named Sheldon J. "Shel" Kaphan. Since graduating from Stanford, Kaphan had made a name for himself as a great engineer, however, his choices in jobs hadn't worked out as he hoped. Since leaving his last position, Kaphan was in the same type of spot as Bezos and was looking for someone to go into business with. The other name Bezos received was a buddy of Kaphan's named Herb. Bezos didn't waste any time in tracking down Herb and Kaphan. He decided to head to Santa Cruz where he could officially meet the two potential business partners.

The three men started talking and soon realized that they all had a similar dream: they wanted to start their own online business. They also realized that all three of them felt there was a lot of potential in the internet and this was indeed the future of the world. Unknown to Bezos at the time, Kaphan and Herb were taking this just as seriously as Bezos did. Just like Bezos was making sure they would be the greatest business partners for his company, they were making sure Bezos was going to be a great business partner.

When asked about meeting Bezos for the first time, Kaphan has told reporters that he thought he was a highly intelligent and energetic man who had a high ability to succeed in business. Both him and Herb liked and believed in Bezos immediately as they felt he had this natural gift when it came to business. On top of this, they also believed that he had a great mind for the business world and would be able to carry his own business far into the future.

After conversing with both Kaphan and Herb over a period of time, Bezos asked the men if they would be interested in coming to work for him. At the time, Bezos remained honest about what he could do for them now and what he wanted to do for them when his company was established. By this time, Herb and Kaphan had become so excited about the potential to work with Bezos that they jumped at the opportunity. Even though there were still many unanswered questions, such as where Bezos was going to base his company, Herb started looking for places in California. However, Bezos quickly informed him that they would probably not be staying in California.

As Bezos continued to make his plans for the company, he kept in contact with his new employees and informed them of his thought process and any decisions he had made. Together, the three would discuss it, but ultimately, it was Bezos' company which meant it was his choice. The other two understood this.

At the time, most entrepreneurs were moving to Silicon Valley. While this area did come up on Bezos' list of locations, he did not feel that would be the best move. He wanted to pick the perfect spot for a company which was going to grow along with the internet. No matter where Bezos looked, he knew he had three main points for whatever place he chose. First, he wanted to find a city that held one of the warehouses for the book companies he would be buying his books from. By remaining close to the warehouse, Bezos and his team could purchase the book customers bought from them quickly. Second, he wanted a location that held other software programmers. Finally, he wanted to make sure that the whole state had a low population because this state would need to pay taxes on the books Bezos sold.

He then started looking at where Microsoft is located, which is in Seattle, Washington. As he looked into this area, Bezos noticed that Seattle was quickly becoming an area of the world at the forefront of the future wave of technology and the internet. It was at this moment Bezos brought up the idea of making his company's home base Seattle. Not only did Seattle have the three points that Bezos wanted when he was looking for a location, but the city also held many other advantages for a business like Amazon.

In fact, because of Microsoft, Seattle was a magnet for people who were starting their own technology companies. For example, Adobe Systems and Nintendo were starting to find their way into Seattle due to the Microsoft environment. On top of this, other tech companies, which were considered to mimic other major tech companies were starting to move their way in Seattle.

After talking to Herb and Kaphan, Bezos made the official decision. He would pack up his family, which included his wife MacKenzie at the time, and leave for Seattle. There, the couple would find a place to live and Bezos would immediately start working on setting up his company. At this point, Bezos' start of Amazon became a little less settled. Whether it was because Bezos was known to be a risk taker and just decided to pack up and head to Seattle without really looking for a home first or because this history just isn't written down yet is uncertain. But, what is known is that when Bezos and his wife got to Seattle, they did eventually settle in a house and this address would become the first location for Amazon.

When Bezos called Herb and Kaphan with the official word for them to start heading to Washington, both men started to rethink going into business with Bezos. In fact, Herb would never make the move and eventually dropped the idea of working with Bezos completely. Kaphan, however, would start heading towards Seattle, though he had no idea where he was going to be living or even when he would meet up with Bezos. All he knew is that Bezos and MacKenzie were already on their way to Seattle and he had to hurry up and start packing for his own move.

Later in his life, Kaphan would admit to reporters that he wasn't happy with Bezos' decision. While it obviously worked out well, he felt that Silicon Valley was the best place for the company. However, it was Bezos company and, therefore, it would be in Seattle. He also admitted that knowing the decided city was Seattle made him rethink joining in on the business. He really didn't want to leave California, yet he also saw this as a stepping stone for himself. He wanted to put programming on his resume. Furthermore, Kaphan didn't officially move to Seattle until later. In fact, he only packed what he absolutely needed and left most of his belongings in his home in Santa Cruz.

While Herb didn't make the move and left the company behind, Kaphan would go on to play a very important part in the company's history and growth. He would not only help Bezos grow the company at the beginning when Amazon officially went public, but he would also help Bezos over the course of five years. Kaphan was Amazon's first official employee.

A Brief History of the Growth of Amazon

A few months later, on July 16, 1995, Bezos founded Cadabra, which was basically an online bookstore. The name came from a conversation Bezos had on his way to Seattle with a Seattle attorney. The attorney told Bezos that it was like he was working on creating a magical store and, therefore, thought of the abracadabra, but he knew this would not work out for a name. Therefore, the attorney told Bezos to shorten it to Cadabra. While Bezos wasn't really feeling that name, he continued to contact the name of a person, Todd Tarbert, who could help Bezos get his company incorporated. The name chosen for incorporation was Cadabra.

Bezos created the business plans for his new career while on an airplane heading to Seattle from New York. Once home in Seattle, Washington, Bezos opened the store in his garage. The main reason for this was because people in many other states would not have to pay sales tax. Bezos felt that this would catch the attention of customers. He then bought $60 blond wood doors, which he turned into two desks.

It did not take long for Bezos to receive his first order. However, he did not have any stock. Instead, he would receive the money from the customer and then go purchase the book from a supplier and then ship the item. Unfortunately, this quickly became a problem. When Bezos opened the store, he wanted the widest selection of books possible. Therefore, people were purchasing classic and rare books which could sometimes not be purchased quickly through other stores. On top of this, Bezos and his two-man team received more orders than they predicted. In fact, in the first week, they received $12,000 from orders, shipping over $800 worth of books. Their second week, they had little time to catch up with

$14,000 in sales and half of that being shipped.

Later, he changed the name from Cadabra to Amazon. He decided on this name for two reasons. First, it reminded him of the Amazon River, which is the largest river in the world. Second, he knew with an "A" name, his company would be at the top of the retail list. On top of this, the name was easy to spell and pronounce, which are two important factors when it comes to naming a business. Bezos states that many people don't realize how important it is to make sure people can not only pronounce but also spell the name. It helps people remember the name of a business immensely.

At first, Bezos didn't truly believe that Amazon would become successful. In fact, he told many people that he thought the failure rate for Amazon was at about 70%. While Amazon started as an online bookstore, Bezos always planned on expanding the products he would sell. However, he also knew that he had to do this strategically. He felt that adding more items on Amazon could cause more harm than good. First, he felt it would make bankruptcy a higher possibility. On top of this, Bezos felt that the online world wasn't exactly ready for much more than a bookstore, however, he also knew that it would soon be ready.

Within the first month, Bezos' new company sold books to about 45 countries. On top of this, the gross monthly earnings were about $20,000. Still, Bezos was not sure that his business would become a success. However, he also knew that he had to continue to grow with his business. Therefore, Bezos started to hire more people to help Amazon grow and succeed.

In 1997, Bezos officially incorporated Amazon.com. Slowly, he started increasing the items he sold and within three years, took Amazon public with an IPO or initial public offering of $18 per share. However, many investors did not take Amazon's stock as they were not sure the company would be able to last long. In the end, this became a bigger blessing for Amazon than anyone realized as the company was able to escape the market crash which started in 1997 and lasted until 2001.

Amazon then started looking at expanding into the cyber world. This became more important when Barnes & Noble launched its own website at the end of 1997. Not only did Bezos and his team look into securing out-of-print and rare books, but they also looked to take their online bookstore into other areas of the world. For example, in 1998 an online British bookstore known as Bookpages became Amazon UK.

Even though Amazon continued to grow in the mid to late 1990s. Bezos continued to believe that his company would eventually go bankrupt. He felt that other online stores would eventually swallow Amazon up as the online world continued to grow. However, Bezos would soon learn that his fear would not come true, especially when he started selling music and movies on Amazon.

In 1998, Bezos continued to expand his company and started to take a more aggressive approach with the money he had made the year prior. At the same time, Amazon was becoming more popular. This not only brought more shoppers but also more critics. Bezos read and listened to all the criticism he received about Amazon. He not only read the good feedback from the customers but also the negative feedback from market critics. They stated there was no way a small and newer company would be able to hold its own for very long. Bezos read reviews that told him many other stores, such as Barnes and Noble, were getting into the online market and these stores would cause Amazon to go bankrupt. He read reviews telling him that there was no way Amazon could ever compete with bigger e-commerce retail stores.

However, Amazon kept up with the stores and started to surpass some of them. In fact, in 1999, Bezos learned that his company had not only beaten the competition, but it had also become the number one leader in the e-commerce world. Finally, Bezos realized that Amazon was going to make it in the online world. From there, he continued to not only grow the number of employees but also to grow Amazon's online market. This same year, Bezos would receive one of the highest honors of his career. Not only was he named "King of Cyber Commerce" but Time Magazine also made him "Person of the Year." People felt that Bezos had created the future in Amazon.

It was around this time that Bezos started to look into advertising, but not in the traditional way. Instead, he looked into affiliate marketing, which is when a company can earn a commission by promoting someone else's company. For example, Yahoo supported Amazon by directing every visitor to Amazon. In response, if the person bought something, Amazon would give Yahoo an 8% commission on all the sales. Once this type of marketing started, Amazon's sales increased dramatically.

In 2001, Amazon came in at about $1 billion in revenue and a $5 million profit. It was at this moment when people started to believe that it wasn't Amazon that was bringing all the profit, but the man behind the idea. People started to take a closer look at Bezos and noticed that while he did believe that Amazon could fail, he also started to find successful trends years before other people saw it. This told many investors, critics, competition, and customers that Bezos had a natural gift for business. Furthermore, Bezos' wealth stood at about $10.5 billion.

Many people, including Bezos, believe that one of the reasons Amazon became so successful is because of how he conducts his business. For example, unlike most businesses, he does not allow his employees to submit their reports through a

PowerPoint presentation. Bezos states that all people do with PowerPoint is look at the numbers and state facts through bullet points. Instead, he makes his employees write reports so they can think critically and analyze their results. This system has proven to be successful and has helped establish the great corporate culture Amazon is known for today.

Around 2000-2002, Amazon would take a financial hit. Not only because of lawsuits but also because of the market itself. The price of their shares dropped from $106 to $15, but because of Amazon's growing market and Bezos' business leadership, Amazon made it through this struggle.

Not too long after Amazon had to lay off over a thousand employees, Bezos launched the Amazon Marketplace. This allowed the company to take a commission from other business' sales. Furthermore, Bezos and his team continued to find ways to diversify Amazon as Bezos knew that one of the best ways to keep increasing Amazon's sales was to get more items in the door so they can be sold. On top of this, he knew that the more Amazon changed, the more people would discuss the company.

2005 started off as a busy year for Amazon. Not only did the company obtain a Chinese online bookstore known as Joyo for $75 million, but Amazon Prime was introduced. This program started with 1 million items which would arrive at their destination in two days. The main purpose of this program was to enhance customer satisfaction. Bezos knew that people hated waiting for their items, which meant that some would continue to shop at local stores rather than on Amazon. Therefore, Bezos thought that having a faster shipping program would increase Amazon's sales. Today, Amazon Prime is one of the company's biggest programs. Millions of members continuously purchase Amazon Prime every year. Furthermore, the program's items continue to grow. Within 15 years, the items grew from 1 million to over 30 million.

In 2005, Amazon announced its new video on demand service, which eventually became known as Amazon Instant Video. In 2011, Amazon had released the Amazon Kindle and then the Kindle Fire HD the following year. By 2012, Amazon made $17 billion in sales, which was a major leap from their $510 thousand in 1995. On top of this, Amazon became one of the few e-commerce websites established during the 1990s to continue its business. Many of the newer sites had failed between 1997 and 1999.

Amazon's Ever Growing Merchandise List

If you look on Amazon today, you will see that the categories are definitely diverse. You can not only buy books but music, movies, groceries, clothing, and so much more. However, all these items did not come out at once. In fact, Amazon has continued to add new items every 1-3 years since 1995. Below is a look at what items came into Amazon's warehouses and when.

- 1998 – DVDs and CDs

- 1999 – Electronics, toys, games, and video games

- 2000 – Amazon Marketplace, which allowed third-party sellers to place anything which could be shipped or delivered electronically on Amazon.

- 2002 – Clothing and Amazon's cloud computing, a web service.

- 2003 – Jewelry

- 2004 – Shoes

- 2005 – Amazon Prime and Video on demand

- 2006 – Amazon Fresh

- 2007 – Amazon Kindle e-Reader, and Kindle Direct Publishing

- 2008 – Amazon video games

- 2009 – Amazon Publishing and Amazon Basics

- 2010 – Amazon Studios

- 2011 – Amazon Kindle Fire, Amazon Flow, and Amazon Locker

- 2013 – Amazon Art

- 2014 – Amazon Echo and Amazon Fire Phone

- 2015 – Amazon's first brick-and-mortar store established in Seattle.

- 2018 – Amazon Go

As you can see, Amazon has not only grown in the types of merchandise it sells but also in the services it offers. While a few of these services, such as the Amazon Fire Phone, didn't do well; the majority of services perform exceptionally well. Furthermore, Amazon now competes with nearly every store imaginable, except maybe a gas station. Amazon competes with Apple and Google through their technology along with the more common retail stores such as Target. On top of this, Amazon also competes with online streaming specialists such as Hulu and Netflix.

However, Amazon's growth does not even stop here as it's also acquired several other businesses over the years:

- 1998 – Bookpages.com, PlanetAll, and Exchange.com.

- 2008 – A digital audiobooks provider known as Audible.

- 2009 – An e-reader app known as Stanza.

- 2009 – An e-commerce footwear called Zappos.

- 2011 – An e-commerce retail store which focused on household items, beauty, and baby products called Quidsi and Lovefilm International, an overseas streaming service in Europe.

- 2012 – Kiva Systems, which is a robotics company.

- 2013 – Twitch, a streaming company.

- 2015 – A chip designer based in Israel known as Annapurna Labs and Aws Elemental.

- 2017 – Whole Foods Market and Souq, which is basically Amazon in the Middle East.

- 2018 – A smart doorbell camera operator known as Ring.

Struggles Still Persist

No matter how well Amazon did, there were still struggles that Bezos, his team, and the company had to endure. For example, Amazon started to deal with a lot of lawsuits, most of which came about because of other major retailers such as Barnes & Noble, Walmart, and various Fortune 500 corporations.

One of Amazon's first lawsuits came from Barnes & Noble, who sued the company for claiming that Amazon was the "world's largest bookstore." However, in a sense, this turned out to be both a positive and negative for Amazon. This was a negative because not only is a lawsuit negative media attention, but Amazon didn't have any proof to back up their claims, other than that they had a wide variety of books available for purchase. However, this also became a positive for Amazon because the news of this lawsuit came just days before Amazon's stocks went on the market at $18. All this put Amazon on people's radar. Whether they were thinking about buying a book or stocks, Amazon saw a growth of about 900% in revenues after this lawsuit.

Unfortunately, all of the lawsuits would leave Amazon having to pay a total of $1.4 billion in 2000. Because of this, Bezos and other executives were forced to lay off over 1,000 workers and find new cost-reduction strategies to help keep the company growing. Fortunately, this downturn didn't last too long for Amazon as the company made $5.1 million by the end of that year.

However, like anything else, Bezos took this struggle as a learning experience. Through the new cost-reduction strategies, he learned that the company could continue to save money, which would increase its net worth.

Why Amazon?

Many people question why Amazon became successful over many other e-commerce stores at the time. With how quickly the internet was growing, new e-commerce stores were coming together at a fast rate. Many people point to a few reasons that may explain Amazon's success.

Bezos' Remains Realistic

Bezos knew there was a chance Amazon could fail and he remained realistic about that chance for years. Even when the numbers increased rapidly within the company's first month, Bezos still mentioned that the failure rate of the company was at 70%. While Bezos' expectations have changed over the last couple of decades, he does his best to remain realistic.

Bezos' Natural Talent in Business

If you haven't already realized that Jeff Bezos has a natural gift when it comes to business, you will by the end of this book. With an interest in business since he was a child, Bezos often read books which would help him discover the business world. On top of this, he thought critically about everything he read. There was never a moment in his childhood where he wasn't learning and forming his own thoughts and beliefs on the subject.

Along with his knowledge, Bezos seems to have a natural entrepreneur mind. He not only thinks carefully about his next business decision, but he also follows his own path. He won't always do what other businessmen are doing, even if it is working for them, for example, he doesn't focus on the competition but the customers.

Bezos Embraced New Technology

When Amazon opened computers had already been around for a while, however, the internet was new. Many people were afraid to put their business online because they weren't positive that the internet would become successful. Bezos, on the other hand, was willing and ready to take the risk. In fact, Bezos imagined a future run by computers and the online world. He knew that this was the exact direction businesses would need to go in order to succeed.

One of the First to Establish a Credit Card Business Online

Not only was Bezos one of the first to take his retail business online, but he was one of the first to accept credit cards. Of course, many other retail giants such as Target would quickly add this feature, but Amazon received the benefits of being one of this first. This included being able to make sales that other retail stores could not online as they didn't accept payments through credit cards.

Amazon's Internal Factors Grew with its Customer Base

Bezos kept the internal workings of Amazon small until he needed it to grow. For example, he didn't hire a large number of employees until his sales proved he needed to. The same went with Amazon's headquarters. While the company was stated to be "Earth's Largest Bookstore" from its beginning, its headquarters were in Bezos' garage until he needed to move to a bigger location.

The Success of Amazon is Still Growing

Recently, Bezos hit another milestone when it came to his ever-growing company. In 2018, Amazon became the second company in the United States to hit a value of more than $1 trillion. The only other company in United States history to reach this type of value is Apple. Later, Forbes went on to say that Bezos has a net worth of about $110 billion. This makes him one of the richest men in modern day history.

Chapter 5: Blue Origin

After his valedictorian speech, Bezos gave the *Miami Herald* an interview where he talked more about his interest in space. He stated that one of his goals was to be able to preserve Earth. However, in order to do this, he had to find a way to get people into space. He stated that he would be able to establish colonies in space where people can live just as they could on Earth. They would be able to build homes, hotels, parks, restaurants, grocery stores, and anything else which is needed in a community. Children could go to school in space, where they can learn just as they do on Earth. In fact, Bezos felt they could learn more because space would give people a new direction for education.

No matter where Bezos' career path took him, whether it was Fitel or Amazon, his love of space stayed. This became more obvious to the world when Bezos announced in the fall of 2000 that he had founded a spaceflight company which he named Blue Origin. Even though the company started in 2000, for its first few years, barely anything was said about Blue Origin. While people continued to talk about Bezos and Amazon, they nearly forgot about Blue Origin. However, this has all changed within the last decade.

People started to remember Bezos' space company after he purchased a large tract of land in Texas. The purpose of this land was to give the company a location where they could test and launch. On top of this, Bezos had another plan for Blue Origin. Not only did he want to expand what the world knows about outer space, but he also wants to make the whole process more affordable. Additionally, Bezos wants anyone to be able to travel into space. While there will still be a training program for people who chose to go into space, along with making sure they can safely travel, the program guidelines and requirements will not be as strict as NASA's program.

Once Bezos purchased the land in 2006, Blue Origin continued to grow. One of the first steps was to test the aircraft. Unfortunately, not all the tests would be successful. In September 2011, Bezos and his team sent an aircraft prototype for a test run. Even though the test flight was short, the prototype crashed. Fortunately, no one was hurt and this wasn't a testing aircraft which needed to be controlled by a human. Of course, this did not hurt Bezos' determination for his space quest as he runs Blue Origin similar to how he runs Amazon: you will make mistakes, learn from the mistakes, and use the mistakes to figure out something better. Of course, when the crash hit the media outlets, people started wondering what would become of Blue Origin. However, many news articles were quick to state that, while the company has seen little light in the news, they have made amazing progress when it comes to space exploration.

A couple of years later, Bezos decided to meet with another space enthusiast, Richard Branson, who is the chairman of Virgin Galactic and also a billionaire. Bezos met with Branson so they could discuss strategies for commercial spaceflight.

In 2015, Blue Origin made the news again when Bezos announced that the company was working on a new spacecraft, which they would send into space in the distant future. While Bezos spoke like this would take a couple of years, it was later that year when the Blue Origin team sent their New Shepard space rocket 329,839 feet (100.5 kilometers) into the air before the rocket successfully landed in the western part of Texas. This was a huge success for the company.

A year later, Bezos decided to bring a variety of people into the Blue Origin headquarters so they could get a sneak peek at the facility. Part of the reason Bezos did this was that he had seen how interested the media had become in his company. Therefore, he allowed journalists to come in so they could interview him about the company and photograph the headquarters. Bezos felt that doing this would foster more public interest in getting into space.

In 2017, New Shepard saw the light of day again as it went on another test run. This time, it held dummy passengers so the Blue Origin team could see what would happen if a human flew and landed in the spacecraft. While Bezos and his team realized that they would still have work to do to make New Shepard safer for human travel, he also stated that it could be as soon as late 2018 when they send their first human into space.

Throughout the rest of 2017 and into 2018, the company built more spacecraft like New Shepard and continued to test each one. First each New Shepard would receive a non-dummy test, then a dummy test, and finally a commercial passenger operations test. During testing, Bezos raised the price of tickets for the New Shepard from $200,000 to $300,000 per person. On top of this, about a billion dollars in Amazon shares started to go towards funding Blue Origin.

As of the writing of this book, no person has been sent into space through Blue Origin. However, Bezos stated in May 2019, that the company is one step closer to sending its first customers into space. They are still focusing on test flights, however, each flight proves that the company is getting closer to reaching one of their goals.

Chapter 6: The Washington Post and Other Adventures

While most people think of Amazon or Blue Origin when they hear the name Jeff Bezos, he has taken on other business ventures. One of these is recently purchasing The Washington Post. He has also taken on several other smaller businesses, whether it is becoming a share in the business or just helping support the business. Because of all this hard work and innate knowledge of how to be a great businessman, Bezos has quickly worked his way up to the top of the financial ladder in the United States. For example, in 2017 Bezos became the top billionaire on Forbes' "Real Time Billionaires List." A year later, Bezos officially became the richest man in the world, pushing Bill Gates, who had held that spot for at least 18 years, down to number two.

Because Bezos' wealth has increased so quickly, people have wondered exactly how much he makes in an hour. Early in 2019, the Business Insider, an online business news source which Bezos supports, broke down what he makes annually, per month, per day, and per hour. They started with Bezos' net worth at the time, which was $137 billion and determined his most current annual net worth to be about $78.5 billion. This means he makes about $6.5 billion a month, $1.5 billion a week, over $215 million a day, and almost $9 million an hour.

Of course, Bezos' wealth does not just come from Amazon and Blue Origin. It also comes from investing, The Washington Post, and many other business ventures that Bezos is a part of. Here is a look at a few of them and how they came to be one of Bezos' business passions.

The Washington Post

You might think between Amazon and Blue Origin, Bezos is too busy to take on other business adventures. However, Bezos feels that there is always room for one more business venture.

In early August 2013, Bezos announced that he had purchased The Washington Post from Katharine Graham Weymouth, whose family had owned the business for years. Through establishing a limited liability holding company known as Nash Holdings, Bezos purchased the newspaper for $250 million.

By this time, The Washington Post had been going for about 140 years. However, the future outlook of the newspaper showed that it was going downhill. It didn't take long for Bezos to make his first change to the newspaper as one of the first things he noticed was the governance of The Washington Post. First, when it came to shareholders, the company needed to please them in a way which would maximize profits and limit loss. While this is typical for companies, what was going on with The Washington Post was they didn't focus on Wall Street's demands for profit. Therefore, when Bezos took over, he quickly noted this and made strict changes and a new organization in this area. At the same time, he also noted that the company was understaffed, so he increased staff as he felt this would help production. He didn't just hire more journalists and editors, but also more technical employees and engineers.

From there, Bezos started to instill a mix of motivation and confidence within the employees and what they could do for The Washington Post. He used the same techniques he does with his Amazon employees. These factors quickly helped increase the traffic that the post saw on a daily basis. Furthermore, Bezos didn't change everything. For example, Bezos didn't change higher positions within the post. Martin Baron, the Executive Editor, and Shailesh Prakash, the Chief Information Officer, remained on staff. Bezos worked with these two in order to figure out the best changes for the company.

Technology also became a bigger part of The Washington Post. Bezos felt that at the time, the post wasn't doing everything they could when it came to technology. Not only did Bezos work with Prakash to find new avenues in technology for the post's visitors, but technology remains one of the main missions when it comes to the company. Instead of looking at how journalism can help technology, Bezos focused on how technology can help journalism.

Finally, Bezos and Prakash incorporated the Barbell Approach, which is when The Washington Post became a part of Apple New and Google's Accelerated Mobile Pages. This brought the news from the post out instantly through their Facebook page.

In March 2014, he took off the online paywall for local newspaper subscribers in Minnesota, Texas, and Hawaii. Two years later, Bezos made other changes by reinventing the newspaper as more of a technology and media company in order to keep up with the times. When he did this, Bezos reconstructed the newspaper's analytic software, digital media, and mobile platform.

Throughout 2014 and into 2015, Bezos did what he could to help build up the company's moral and turn the company in the right direction. The steps Bezos took to complete this process helped as by the fall of 2015, The Washington Post had more online traffic than the New York Times by around a million visitors. While the New York Times had 65.8 million internet visitors, the Washington Post received 66.9 million. On top of that, this was nearly 60% more visitors for the Washington Post compared to 2014.

When Bezos bought The Washington Post, the newspaper was not performing financially well. However, after Bezos' latest changes, he had taken the newspaper out of the red and it is now making money in order to sustain itself.

Of course, not everyone was impressed with the positive change that happened within The Washington Post. In fact, The New York Times wrote an article, which Bezos decided to respond to, about whether the changes he made were appropriate for the workplace. This company was concerned about the direction that Bezos was taking journalism as a whole as his decisions didn't just affect the post but also other newspaper entities. Furthermore, the article didn't agree with Bezos' values when it came to how he treated his employees and handled his businesses. While Bezos read the article from the New York Times, he responded with the basic fact that this article was not going to change the way he ran his businesses, especially Amazon. In fact, Bezos stated, that he believed other companies should look at Amazon's policies as they would help that company prosper.

Bezos Expeditions

Another way that Bezos has made his billions is through investing his money. In fact, he was one of the first people to invest in Google when he purchased stock for $250,000 during 1998. Today, this stock is worth over $3.1 billion.

Bezos has admitted to using this stock to help fund certain parts of his other business adventures. For example, he uses Bezos expeditions to startup firms such as an Airbnb, an online hospitality service provider and marketplace, and a transportation program known as Uber Technologies. At the same time, Bezos has used money from this area in order to support his businesses Amazon, Blue Origin, and the Washington Post.

Chapter 7: A Work and Family Life Balance

While Bezos recently divorced from his wife, Mackenzie, in the beginning of 2019, this does not mean that he was unable to do his best in balancing his work and family life. Bezos met Mackenzie Tuttle when he was working for D. E. Shaw in 1992. Tuttle also worked for the company and the two started dating, getting married in 1993. The following year, they decided to move to Seattle, Washington, which is when Bezos took one of the biggest risks of his life and started Amazon in their garage.

Together, the couple has four children, three of whom are biological, two sons and a daughter. They also have another daughter, who they adopted from China. For the many years the Bezos' were married, both sides did everything they could to make sure they were each supporting their partner. For example, during Amazon's early years, MacKenzie worked as an accountant. She then left her post to start focusing on starting a family and writing. However, once the couples' third child arrived, she realized she had very little time for writing as she wanted to focus on being the best mother she could be. With her decision to pause her writing, her husband supported her.

Furthermore, he also supported her when she decided to pick up writing again as her children were all in school and she found herself with more time on her hands. In order to give his wife the best support, he decided to take time out of his busy day and read the manuscript she had been working on. On top of this, MacKenzie noted, that he provided the best feedback he could, positive and negative, to help her manuscript move forward in the best way.

During his presentations, Bezos is quick to discuss how it is important to have structure within your work and family life. For years, Bezos would wake up early in the morning so he could have breakfast with his family. He did his best to make sure that his mornings were set aside for Mackenzie and their children. In fact, he would rarely schedule meetings until later in the morning because early mornings were reserved for his family.

However, this does not mean that Bezos felt he did this to create a work and personal life balance. In fact, Bezos is open in stating that one piece of advice he gives his new Amazon employees is not to think of work and family as two separate sides of one life. Instead, Bezos believes that you have to connect them and create a circle. Furthermore, he states that this can be accomplished by setting a simple schedule which includes both pieces of your life.

Not only did Bezos make sure mornings were for his family, but he also made sure to set aside time every day to accomplish some household chores, such as the dishes. He believes that if you stick to your schedule, don't set up too many meetings, and don't stress yourself out with trying to find the best professional and family life balance you will be able to achieve all your goals.

One of the biggest reasons Bezos states no one should aim for the work and family balance is because this makes it feel like you have to make a tradeoff between the two. In an interview with the Business Insider Bezos stated "I get asked about work-life balance all the time. And my view is, that's a debilitating phrase because it implies there's a strict trade-off."[6]

Bezos believes that by looking at his work and personal life as integrated parts, he has not only been able to remain happy, but he also energized. He claims there is rarely a time where he goes into work feeling drained of energy or goes home at the end of the day feeling tired. He states that by limiting the stress of feeling the need to find the balance, he has been able to keep his outlook and energy positive in both environments.

_____

[6] Bernard, 2019.

Bezos continues to support his belief of creating a circle by stating you just never want to turn into that person who becomes so emotionally drained that you drag other people down with you. He fully believes that the type of energy you put out in your environment will be the type of energy you get back. Therefore, if you come in to work happy, your co-workers will be happy.

Bezos attributes his success in life to his belief in creating a circle and not a balance. He fully believes that if he was to take on the stress of trying to find the perfect balance, he could have easily let that stress cloud his mind. In return, this could affect his decisions at work and at home. Therefore, if you have a dream of becoming an entrepreneur like Jeff Bezos, you will want to think about how you can integrate your home and work life instead of trying to find a strict balance.

Chapter 8: Business Start-up Tips from Jeff Bezos

In the following chapters, you will not only read some of the best start-up tips Bezos gives entrepreneurs for their business, but you will also read about some of Bezos' business lessons and receive everyday advice from one of the world's richest men.

Before Bezos' started his own business, Amazon, he worked various jobs. While he found work that he was interested in, he knew he wasn't passionate about the work. For him, it was a paycheck. Bezos was getting married to his fiancé and he knew that one day they would have a family. This meant that he knew they needed money not only coming in to help pay the bills, groceries, and gas but also money to start building their savings.

As he worked, Bezos realized there was something important missing in his life. As he thought about it, he realized that one of the biggest things he wanted to do - the thing that he was most passionate about - was starting his own business. Therefore, Bezos gave his resignation at his job and with very little money in his pocket, started his first business, Amazon.

With everyone knowing that Bezos started Amazon from nothing into one of the top companies, people often turn to

Bezos for tips on what they should do when starting their own company. Below are some of the tips that Bezos often shares.

1. Get the Best Advice You Can but Also Ignore It

Bezos is always willing to share any type of advice he can about business because he feels that he gives good advice. He tends to give advice through his own experiences and what has worked for his businesses, especially Amazon. He figures that if he was able to build one of the greatest businesses in modern history that he should know how to help other entrepreneurs with their business.

This doesn't mean that Bezos should be the only person you seek advice from. While he is one of the best CEOs in the United States who is willing to help, there are a lot of places where you can seek advice. The trick is, you have to find the best advice that you can for you and the company you want to establish.

At the same time, Bezos states that you also need to know when you should throw away the advice you have been given – even his. In a sense, Bezos states you need to know when you can just toss the rule book to the side and focus on what is best for your company. Get an idea from people who are successful and then do what is right for you. Just because something worked for someone else doesn't mean that this advice is going to work for you.

Bezos often explains this by giving the story of pre-Amazon. Bezos and a couple of other people who were going to start up the business with him went around and talked to other people, such as friends, family, and professionals, about the idea they had. They stated that the idea Bezos had about selling books completely online was a bad investment. No one thought it would work. So, Bezos decided to take the advice they were given and ignore it. They then went on to start the company Bezos imagined.

2. Don't Focus on a Quick Buck

Bezos realizes that many people want to start up a business because they want to make money and they want to make money quickly. He also realizes that many people won't agree with an idea because they feel that it won't make sales in the short-term. Bezos disagrees with this mindset.

While you can make millions off your business, this isn't going to happen quickly. Bezos feels that it is very important for people to remember this. They have to give their company time to grow and prosper. He also states that one way to do this is by not always paying attention to the short-term prospects of your product but the long-term. Like Bezos states, even if he measures an idea and it comes out that it won't help the company make money in the short-term, they still follow through with the idea if in the long-term it can carry the benefits the company needs.

3. You Need to Have Faith

When Bezos decided to start up Amazon, he had a comfortable Wall Street job. However, he also had faith in the idea he had for Amazon. At the same time, he knew little about actually running his own business, little about the internet, and virtually nothing about creating an online business. But, what Bezos did have, was a lot of faith that he could make this company successful.

Today, Bezos looks back on his decision and states that he knew if he didn't jump on the idea he had for Amazon that he would regret it every day of his life. In order to realize this, Bezos imagined himself as an old man and thought back on his life. He thought about his idea and where it could lead him and thought about his life if he didn't follow through with his idea. It was then Bezos came to the realization that he had to act on the idea or he would forever wonder what would have happened.

Of course, now it is easy for Bezos to be happy in his life. His idea worked and became one of the top companies in the world, he loves his work, he is focusing on other business endeavors, and he never has to worry about his finances.

Because of his story, Bezos often supports his employees in taking their own leaps, even if it means that they will leave Amazon. Not only does he encourage his staff to create their own ideas but he also encourages them to follow their own passions. Of course, he gives the same advice to any entrepreneur.

4. Don't Overthink Your Decisions

Bezos has caught himself overthinking before, especially during the early days of Amazon. It's a common trait which many people have, and often reaches its peak when they are focusing on the best decisions for their business. However, Bezos states that you always have to be careful of this and one way to not overthink as an intellectual is by thinking simply.

Remember, Bezos believes in having your customers as your number one, even before your competitors. Therefore, you need to think of your typical audience, who won't understand things like you do. You need to make sure your customers can relate to you and the products you are giving out. If they can't relate, then they aren't going to pay attention to your company or purchase your products. If this happens, your company is going to fail.

Of course, overthinking isn't just something you can stop doing. In fact, it's completely possible that you don't realize you're overthinking. Therefore, it's important to note the signs that mean you're overthinking and learn ways to overcome it.

How to Know You're an Over-thinker

1. You want everything to be perfect. However, nothing is perfect. You can do well in your job or create a great new device that becomes a best seller in your company without making it perfect. As Bezos states, sometimes you take an idea and launch it, just to bring it back to the creative table and make it better. He also states that if you focus on making things perfect right away, there is no way you can move it up in the world. There is no way that you can make it better. There is nothing that you can do with it so people want to buy it five years from now. While it might help your business in the short-term, it won't help in the long-term.

2. Another way to know you are overthinking in your professional life is you get stuck when trying to make your decision. While Bezos and his team take a lot of time to think about decisions, they don't continue to focus on the same decision over and over again as this is overthinking. Instead, they go through their decision-making process and what they come up with is the result of this idea.

3. You find yourself unable to make other decisions. While many people are unaware of this, there is such a thing as decision exhaustion. This happens when you overthink about

one thing. You have focused so much time, energy, and focus on this one decision that you can no longer mentally focus on anything else. This is one reason Bezos won't make decisions at the end of the workday or when he is feeling exhausted. While he tries not to overthink things, he also is completely aware that this can happen without him realizing it. It's a human trait and even the CEOs of major multi-million to billion dollar companies can overthink decisions. Therefore, it's best that when you find yourself with decision exhaustion, you stop thinking about the main cause of your exhaustion and don't try to make other decisions.

4. Another way to know that you are overthinking a decision is the fact that you remain fixated on the small stuff. While the small stuff is important, which is also something Bezos often talks about, you can't give all your attention to the small stuff and ignore the larger items and, most importantly, the bigger picture. When you do this, you are going to miss some valuable information when it comes to your decision and you can find yourself harming your company instead of helping it. Therefore, if you find yourself stuck on the small things, simply move ahead in your decision-making process.

How to Move Beyond Overthinking

If you are going through the above points and realize that you often overthink your decisions, there are many things that can help you overcome overthinking.

1. The first thing you can do you have already completed and that was becoming aware that you are an over-thinker. Once you establish that you tend to overthink things, you can start to catch yourself when you are overthinking and use strategies to help you stop thinking too much about one decision.

2. One strategy you can use is to stop thinking negatively. People often overthink, especially when it deals with their company, because they become concerned about all the things that can go wrong. You don't want to find yourself doing this. Instead, you want to focus on the positives and think of all the things that can go right if you make this decision.

3. Do your best to get rid of your fear. One of the main reasons people think to overthink things is because they hang on to their fear of what can happen. Bezos is a strong believer in making sure you don't let fear take over any decision you make. In fact, he wants people to become as fearless as possible. One of the reasons Bezos feels this way is because it can help people stop overthinking.

4. Sometimes you need to set a timer or a deadline. If you find yourself overthinking nearly every decision you make, it might help you to set a deadline or use a timer. Only allow yourself so long to make your decision and then once your time runs out, focus on your next decision. For example, when Bezos sets up a meeting where decisions are going to be made,

they are made within that meeting. He doesn't focus on making any of these decisions outside of that meeting. They are made within the meeting and then he moves on to the next task or decision.

How Does Jeff Bezos Make Decisions?

One of the biggest things beginning entrepreneurs wonder is how Bezos makes decisions within his companies. Bezos spent time writing up a shareholder letter with just this information a couple of years ago. In this letter, Bezos stated that are two main things that you need to focus on to make sure you're not spending too much time on one decision. The first point is you need to make the decision with at least 70% of the information you wish you had. The second point is you have to realize that nearly every decision you make is reversible.

Bezos wants people to remember that when making decisions, the majority of decisions have a two-way door, which means they are reversible. Bezos then asks why anyone would spend so much time focusing on one decision when you can reverse your decision later. On top of this, when the decision is reversed, there is hardly any type of loss or suffering to go along with it. You simply reverse the decision and go from there. He also states that you don't want to focus on the fact that you made the right or wrong decision. People make the wrong decisions and mistakes on a daily basis, it is nothing to regret. In fact, Bezos is a strong believer in not focusing on regrets.

When you are making a decision, Bezos states that you should quickly think of all the information you don't have which would be helpful in your decision-making process. Furthermore, he advises that if you wait for more than 70% of your desired information you are most likely overthinking your decision. Throughout all the decision he has made over the years, he feels that 70% is the best number.

Bezos also states that as you make decisions, you will start to realize what the good decisions are and what the bad decisions are. He believes that this comes naturally as you continue to grow along with your company.

Eventually, You Will Throw Away the Organizational Chart

In nearly every business, there is something called an organizational chart. This chart tells other employees who the CEO is, who this person supervises, and who your supervisor is. Basically, it is the ladder of the company which places each person where they sit on the company's hierarchy. While Bezos states that you might create an organizational chart with your company, you will eventually throw it away. It's not that it won't matter anymore, it's simply the fact that you won't need it.

Bezos believes that one of the greatest things about decisions and working as a team is that this overruled the organizational chart. While the company will still have a CEO and managers which will be ahead of some other employees, this doesn't mean that everyone doesn't have their own weight when it comes to the company as a whole. In fact, Bezos doesn't care where an employee would sit if he still had an organizational chart when it comes to Amazon, he is willing to listen to anyone's ideas as you never know who has the next great service or product when they walk in the doors.

Establish a Hiring Bar

Amazon's hiring bar is extremely important to CEO Jeff Bezos. He believes that through a few well-selected questions, you will be able to find the right person for your business. On top of this, he also states that he would rather take the time to interview dozens of people and not hire any of them than take his chance on hiring the wrong person. Just like the right person can help build a company, the wrong person can help tear a company down. Therefore, Bezos expresses that whenever you are focusing on starting up your own company, you establish a hiring bar and you don't allow yourself to hire below your bar, you hire above your bar.

After interviewing a potential new employee, Bezos takes the time to ask himself three main questions about the person he just met. These questions have been something Bezos has asked himself since he started hiring people to work for him at Amazon and they are questions he still considers today.

1. "Will this person raise the average level of effectiveness of the group they're entering?"[7] When Bezos asks himself this question, he is getting an idea of what this person will bring to his company. Of course, the guidelines he sets for this are not the same guidelines he had 20 years ago or even 10 years ago. Bezos believes that the more your company grows, the higher you will need to raise the hiring bar for any area within your company. When he looks at the guidelines, one of the things he looks at is the 14 leadership principles that the company uses every day. These principles are:

1. Customer obsession is the top leadership principle because this is number one when it comes to Amazon. Whoever Bezos decides to hire, he needs to make sure that they can start with the customer and then work backward in order to give the customer exactly what is needed or wanted. On top of that, the new hire needs to be able to earn and keep the trust of the customer as any customer which loses trust in any member of the Amazon team is not happy and, worse, will stop

---

[7] Montag, 2018.

purchasing items from Amazon.

2. When Bezos looks to hire a new leader for his Amazon team, he needs to find someone that is right in a lot of things the person does. When he looks for this quality, Bezos is looking for someone who will work towards disconfirming his own belief as then he knows that they have one quality it takes to be a good leader. Furthermore, the person needs to have good instincts and often focus on these gut feelings when making a decision.

3. The person takes ownership and is willing to think in a long-term direction. Even if the short-term doesn't look like it will give the company the best results, he is still willing to go forth with the idea because it can help the company in the long-term. He will never sacrifice long-term for short-term outcomes. You will never hear this person say that a certain task is not his job, instead, he will do whatever needs to be done because he is an owner and takes pride in the company overall and not just his area.

4. The person is not afraid of a challenge or confrontation, even if it's with Bezos. In fact, Bezos often welcomes challenges from his employees because he knows that this employee is going to help take the company in the best direction possible. Bezos knows

this is a great quality to have because leaders are people who won't back down because someone tells them to, instead, they work on forming their own questions and figuring out results. Furthermore, this trait tells Bezos that once the decision is made, this person is going to put all his effort into making the idea a reality.

5. Bezos also looks for leaders who can be frugal. If people can create something with less, then they are able to develop things without needing a lot of options. This also shows that the person is resourceful and self-sufficient.

6. Bezos also looks for people who can be respectful to everyone and in any type of situation, even when they are uncomfortable. They also listen very well to other people and speak honestly. They can sometimes make a person feel like she is the only one that matters even if they are talking to a whole group of people. For Bezos, this is one of the traits of a strong leader he would want working for Amazon.

7. Another trait of a leader Bezos looks for is they not only try to better themselves every day but they also try to help other people. A leader will never leave someone behind, especially from his team. Instead, he will take the time to make sure all members are where they need

to be in order to get the work done. When a leader is given a promotion, he will put more effort into his work.

8. Bezos believes that a leader will always not only work to improve himself but also continue to learn. A leader feels like he needs to learn in order to improve everything around him. Furthermore, the more he learns, the more ideas he can create to improve the company as a whole.

9. Not only do leaders understand the importance of being pioneering but they also understand the importance of being simple. A leader will always work with the members of his team in order to invent something new. On top of that, the leader will make sure that all team members keep in mind who they are inventing for and, therefore, need to make sure it remains simple. Furthermore, a leader realizes that there are times the creation might be misunderstood and this is fine.

10. Bezos also looks for someone who wants the best. He wants to find a leader who not only has high standards for himself but also for his team members. The leader will also work to improve his high standards and make sure that these standards grow along with the company.

11. Leaders will not believe there is anything they cannot do and this is an important factor when Bezos looks to hire a new Amazon team member. He wants people who are comfortable performing any task from hiring their own team members to making sure their area remains clean. They will not only perform any job but also be able to connect at any level not only within their department but with any company.

12. Bezos looks for someone who will rise to any occasion, even if he finds that there are obstacles he has to deal with in order to produce the best results. Getting the best results at any cost is essential when working as a leader within the Amazon empire.

13. Bezos is not afraid to think big and he looks for this trait in his leaders as well. In fact, he wants to hire people who can think bigger than anyone else. On top of this, Bezos makes sure that his leaders are not afraid to bring their big ideas to him and will never be afraid to bring their ideas to the public.

14. Bezos values leaders who are comfortable with taking risks. If you tend to overthink things, you won't do well working for Amazon because leaders make decisions quickly as they understand every decision can be reversed.

2. The second question Bezos asks himself about a potential hire is whether the person will be admired or not. When he is working with the recruiters for Amazon, Bezos wants them to think if the person they just spoke with could be someone they admire. If the person is, then they go into the potential hire category. If a person is not someone they can see themselves admiring, they are not taken any farther and won't find a position in Amazon. Bezos states of this part of the hiring process, "I've always tried hard to work only with people I admire, and I encourage folks here to be just as demanding. If you think about the people you've admired in your life, they are probably people you've been able to learn from or take an example from."[8]

3. "Along what dimension might this person be a superstar?"[9] This is the third question Bezos asks before going forward with a possible new employee. There are many areas within Amazon and Bezos wants to make sure that the person he might be hiring will not only fit well for the company as a whole but also become a superstar in a certain area. However, with Bezos, this goes beyond just hiring a person for the company. In fact, he likes to hire people with unique talents

---

[8] Montag, 2018.

[9] Montag, 2018

that they can use to help make the day more fun in the office. For example, in the late 1990s, Bezos hired a National Spelling Bee Champion. While this didn't have anything to do with her job, he did like the fact that he could find her at work and randomly ask her to spell a complicated word.

Furthermore, Bezos states that having people with different talents can bring something to the company that no one else can. In fact, it can bring something to the company that other people couldn't imagine. Therefore, you never know what type of personal talent someone has that can help increase the value of the company. Bezos states that leaders always keep an open mind which includes himself.

These three questions that Bezos wrote about back in 1998 are not only still used within Amazon but many other leaders have started to ask themselves these questions as well.

Chapter 9: Business Lessons from Jeff Bezos

Jeff Bezos never got into business with anything but his drive and hope that he would be successful. He never knew what would come out of his entrepreneurship goals, but he knew that he had to give it the best try he could. Since becoming one of the most successful businessmen in the United States, Bezos has taken time to speak to anyone about the lessons he learned through his journey. Not only has he given speeches at college graduations, but he has also gone on his own tours and spoke in a number of communities. Below are several of the business and life lessons that Bezos often discusses.

1. Realize Your Limits

While Bezos is known to take risks in his business adventures, he is also known to realize his limitations. This is an important focus for Bezos as it helps him so he doesn't get too deep into an idea when it's not going to work. On top of this, it allows Bezos to realize not only where his strengths are but also his weaknesses. He knows that if he knows his limits, he will not only learn what he can't do but also what he can do. There are a couple of ways that Bezos learns his limits. One of these ways is by following basic psychology and the other way is by listening to his customers.

The Psychology of Knowing Your Limits

Psychologically, one of the biggest reasons you need to know your limits is because it will help you with your confidence. In return, you will begin to feel successful. In a sense, confidence brings success and this is one personality characteristic that Bezos has had since he was a child. The more Bezos developed robots in his parents' garage, the more he learned what worked and what did not. He started to learn what he could achieve, which helped him establish confidence which grew into his adult years.

Bezos agrees with the psychological business tactic that yes, you should see what you could do. You should try to accomplish goals and tasks as you never know what is going to work and what won't work. However, you also need to know when to stop if something doesn't work. Bezos has followed this rule a lot throughout his business career. He has tried to pursue something which didn't work out for many reasons, such as his customers felt the device would glitch too often. When he finds out that one of his ideas doesn't work, he simply takes it off the market and moves on to the next idea.

This is another way where Bezos follows a psychological business tactic. He doesn't let his failures define his career. He doesn't let it bother him if one of his ideas doesn't work. Furthermore, he doesn't let criticism bother him. Instead, he uses it as a tool to help him grow so he can expand his business the correct way. Like many successful business people such as Steve Jobs and Elon Musk, Bezos realizes that one of the best ways to keep your business successful is to listen to your customers. Without your customers, your business is sure to fail.

Furthermore, knowing your limits will help you with your goals. Every person who runs a successful business is always going to have goals in mind. These goals are going to change as the business grows. The more you realize what your limits are, the more you will be able to establish the right goals for your business. You will be able to adjust your goals when one of your ideas doesn't work in addition to adjusting your goals when an idea does work.

Finally, realizing your limits will help you maintain motivation, self-discipline, and a realistic drive. With these factors, you will be able to not only achieve your goals but be able to further your business in the right direction. Every successful businessman from Warren Buffett to Jeff Bezos holds these personality characteristics as they continue their business ventures.

Listening to Your Customers

Not all businessmen listen to their customers. For example, Steve Jobs never asked his customers what they wanted nor did he really pay attention to any customer reviews. However, this is not how Jeff Bezos runs his business. He is known to pay attention to his customer reviews and has taken things off the market when his customers didn't like the product. Of course, because both of these men became a couple of the most successful businessmen in modern day history, you can note that listening to your customers is more of a personal belief. However, when it comes to Bezos, he feels it is necessary.

In 2018, Bezos gave a talk at the Economic Club of Washington. During his presentation, Bezos stated, "The No. 1 thing that has made us (Amazon) successful by far is obsessive-compulsive focus on the customer as opposed to obsession over the competitor."[10] Bezos went on to discuss how he felt that all business should follow this rule. Bezos stated that he can quickly figure out when a CEO of a company he is talking to follows this rule or tends to obsess over competition instead. When it comes to companies that are thinking of going into business with him, Bezos will only pick the businesses who genuinely focus on customer satisfaction over the competition.

Bezos has always followed this rule and never really worried

---

[10] Premack, 2018.

about competition from other companies. Instead, he just assumed that his company would go bankrupt because of other companies and the growing online market in the late 1990s. This doesn't mean that Bezos changed his tactic to try to make sure Amazon held strong against competitors. Instead, he did something that he felt his competitors didn't do and that was pay attention to what the customers wanted. He would listen to his customers and adjust his business goals and the products he sold through their reviews. Even today, Bezos has not changed this policy.

However, Bezos' customer service policy goes beyond just listening to the customers. In fact, there are several customer service lessons that any person can take away from how Bezos runs his business.

1. *You never want to settle for anything less than 100%.* Sometimes the people within the company feel that as long as the majority of the customers are happy, then they are doing their best. Bezos does not follow this belief. In fact, he discusses in his presentations that no one should ever settle for anything less than 100% in customer satisfaction, not even 99%. Of course, he also states that you need to work towards this goal. For example, in 2011, Bezos stated that Amazon would get all the packages out to 99.9% of their Christmas shoppers before December 25th. The company made this goal, and Bezos discussed how proud he was that everyone made

this goal the following year. However, he also stated that this does not mean his customer service team isn't working towards reaching 100% as they are always aiming for 100% customer satisfaction.

2. *You need to understand your customers, not just listen to them.* There is a difference between listening to people and understanding them. Bezos realizes this and makes sure that his customer service team also understands this. What Bezos means is, anyone can read a customer review or hear customers over the phone. However, it becomes more special when the customer actually feels that the person on the other end of the line truly understands the customer and is trying to help in any way possible. Bezos understands that this philosophy helps the whole situation as both people are going to work together in order to come up with a solution to the problem.

However, Bezos takes this a bit farther. Every year, thousands of Amazon managers and Bezos attend a two-day call center training. Through this training, Amazon managers are able to put the philosophy of understanding over listening to the customer into practice. Every person who works as an Amazon manager, no matter how many years he or she has been in this position, attends the training. Therefore, it's not just training for new managers but also used a refresher course for all the managers and Bezos.

3. *Never be afraid to apologize.* While Amazon has filled its decades focusing on customer satisfaction and genuinely making their customers happy, they have had their share of struggles. One of the most public mistakes Amazon made which caused many customers to become unhappy with their service was when they deleted thousands of copies of *Animal Farm* and *1984*, both written by George Orwell, off peoples' Amazon Kindles as they had been purchased illegally. Of course, once the negative press about Amazon hit the news, many other customers shared their newly-found disinterest in the company.

The Amazon customer service team quickly made a formal apology about the issue. They stated why this happened but also apologized for handling the situation in a distasteful manner. While many customers understood the customer service team's apology, it was Jeff Bezos' personal apology that made many customers start believing in Amazon again. In his apology, Bezos said the way Amazon handled the solution was "stupid, thoughtless, and painfully out of line with our principles."[11] He further stated that the company deserved all the criticism and they would use what they learned here to make better decisions in the future.

---

[11] Premack, 2018.

The customer support that Amazon and Bezos received after his public apology is proof that when you truly apologize, you will continue to receive customer satisfaction. Customers immediately started commenting to Bezos' apology post about how they initially canceled their Kindle subscription, but because of Bezos' thoughtful and honest apology, they would once again become Kindle subscribers. On top of this, the customers stated that they were impressed with the loyalty that Bezos had for the company's customers, which only made them believe in Amazon more than before.

4. *Respect the customer in today's online world*. In his presentations, Bezos talks a lot about how the world has changed. He discusses this by watching the online world transform and becoming a large part of this world. He states that he realizes people don't just tell their few friends they regularly talk to in person or on the phone not to shop or to shop at a store. Instead, they go online and they can tell 8,000 people not to shop at a store. Therefore, Bezos states, it's important to respect the customer in today's online world and not just like you would have 30 years ago.

As a pioneer in e-commerce, Bezos understands that the heavy research people do along with reading previous customer reviews can influence every online business. In fact, Bezos believes, it can easily make or break the business. Therefore, he makes sure that Amazon follows its customer service policies which reflect the e-commerce world. In order to do this, not only do Amazon managers travel with Bezos to a yearly customer service training session, but they also have a very detailed plan on how to handle negative customer reviews. One of the pieces of this plan is that, no matter how frustrated, annoyed, or angry the Amazon representative feels towards the customer, he or she is always to end the conversation with a "thank you."

5. *The empty chair is the most important person in the room.* Early in his career, Bezos brought an empty chair into a meeting with his customer service team and told them that the person sitting in this chair was the most important person in that room, that person was the customer. Since this meeting, Bezos has used the empty chair technique when explaining how important customer satisfaction is to Amazon's policy. The chair is there simply to remind everyone in the room, from Bezos all the way down to customer service employees that the customer is always there. The customer is always watching, listening, and always making notes on everything that Amazon does. The main mission of Amazon is to establish an environment where every employee remembers customer satisfaction is number one and their goal is to make it 100% of the time.

6. *You want to create a customer-centric company.* Bezos stated in an interview, "We don't focus on the optics of the

next quarter; we focus on what is going to be good for customers. I think this aspect of our culture is rare."[12] Several years ago, Amazon established software so they could monitor customer reviews in the most efficient way possible. It doesn't matter what department the customer leaves a review in, the review is going to be placed in Amazon's data which will allow the customer service team to better the company.

Bezos states that creating a customer-centric company has been his goal since his first day and he has never steered away from it. In fact, he has only become more determined to reach 100% customer satisfaction over the years. He states that this data allows him to make the best decisions for the company as he has proof of what the customers want.

7. *You need to serve the needs of the customer.* Bezos spends a lot of time thinking about the best way to give Amazon customers what they need. Instead of creating something and then seeing what customers feel about it, Bezos looks at what his customers need and then works backward in order to give them what they need. In fact, this is how the Kindle Tablet came about. Bezos saw a need to create a device which would allow customers to use Amazon, especially when it came to

---

[12] Premack, 2018.

their purchase of books.

Furthermore, Bezos knows no end when it comes to creating what the customers need. When he was working with his team on developing the Kindle, his finance executive asked Bezos what the budget was for the device. Bezos simply asked the finance executive how much money the company had. On top of this, Bezos doesn't rush any new developments. The Kindle took years to make before the company started selling the device.

2. Continue to Experiment

Since he was a child, Bezos has experimented with machinery and technology. He started creating robots in elementary school and then continued his experimentation as the CEO of Amazon. Since Amazon's beginning, Bezos has focused on coming up with the next great thing.

Sometimes the experiments pay off for Amazon, such as free shipping for orders over $25.00 or Amazon Prime. Both of these experiments have paid off, according to Bezos. While he found that the short-term costs of the free shipping for $25.00 and over didn't work out, he noted that the long-term costs did. Therefore, Amazon decided to continue with free shipping.

When it came to Amazon Prime, Bezos stated that any financial advisor would tell you not to pursue it. Think about it-Amazon receives $79.00 for a customer's year of two-day free shipping. While not all items are included, Amazon takes a chance with Amazon Prime because people can shop often, which would mean Amazon pays for the shipping themselves. However, if people purchase Amazon Prime and only shop a couple of times out of the year, then Amazon makes money. Bezos stated that the bottom line was it made his customers happy. Furthermore, Amazon Prime has worked the whole way around as nearly 4 million people pay for the program every year. So, to Bezos, the program is worth any cost the company has to pay.

However, not all experiments have paid off for Amazon. A few years ago, Bezos and other Amazon executives wondered if advertising would help boost sales. Therefore, a marketing team searched for two of the best television stations to place ads. They found one in Minneapolis, Minnesota and another station in Portland, Oregon. The company then ran ads for a year and a half, which Bezos has admitted was pretty long for an experiment. After the 16 months, Bezos and the other executives determined that advertising wasn't worth the cost. While sales did rise a bit, it wasn't enough to pay for television advertising.

One of the important things to remember about experimenting, according to Bezos, is that you have to measure everything. You have to start measuring with the idea and then continue measuring all the way to the results. You have to measure both short-term and long-term costs. Furthermore, you should measure not only what it would do to the company but also measure what the customers think.

3. Don't Be Afraid to Invent

Bezos is well aware that Amazon often has to take risks. In fact, taking risks is something Bezos has been doing since he started working. Sometimes taking risks means that you spend your money inventing something, even if you aren't sure it will work out.

This is another area where Bezos and other businessmen, such as Steve Jobs differ. If you pay attention to the services and items that Apple offers, there are very few in comparison to everything Amazon offers. All of the categories on Amazon are examples of Bezos and his team's ideas, experiments, and inventions.

When discussing his Amazon team, Bezos makes it clear that he looks to hire people who are comfortable with creating and experimenting. He looks for people who are comfortable with coming up with ideas and will follow through with them. Bezos knows that finding members for his team with this skill is important because Amazon was built on inventing. In fact, Bezos often refers to the members of his team as pioneers in the online store business world.

4. Ask Yourself What Won't Change in the Future

Bezos has often talked about how most people ask him what new thing Amazon will come up with next. He understands why people continuously ask him this question as Amazon seems to always be changing. Bezos likes to make sure things are changing often. However, he also feels that the more important question is the one he is never asked, which is what isn't going to change in the next few years.

Bezos says you need to base your strategy on what isn't going to change in your company. For example, when it comes to Amazon, Bezos knows that people are going to want fast delivery and cheap prices for years to come. Therefore, he uses this as a base when he is working on creating ideas to better his business. Doing this, he is better able to serve his customers by giving them what they want.

5. Don't Be Afraid to Take Risks

Another business lesson that Bezos often discusses is the need to take risks. He will often cite his decision to leave a stable and steady job to follow his dream of creating an online book store, which became Amazon. He tells his audience that this was one of his biggest risks because he was young, married, starting a family, and didn't even know if the business would last. In fact, he was sure it was going to go bankrupt in the end. However, if he wouldn't have taken the risk, he might not have ever been able to live out his dream of owning his own company. Furthermore, chances are the world might not have an online store known as Amazon.

Bezos tells people that before he officially launched Amazon.com in July 1995, the company struggled. However, once Amazon hit the market, he started to see milestones within the first month. For example, not only did the books sell across the United States, but they also sold in 45 countries. Within the first eight weeks, the company reached $20,000 in sales every week.

One of the most recent risks that Amazon took was the Echo. In 2014, Amazon launched a speaker with a voice activation system. At the time, Bezos and his team knew that the Echo was a huge risk because no customer had asked for such a device. They weren't sure how the Echo was going to do on the market. However, within five years, the Echo has gained so much popularity that it ranks up with Amazon Kindle and Amazon Prime. In fact, about 100 million homes have the Echo.

While Bezos and his team wondered how the Echo would do, he stated he wasn't really worried. Bezos believes that failure is a part of the company which allows it to continue growing. For example, they created the Echo from the fire phone, which was a big failure. He also states that the bigger your company becomes, the bigger the failures have to be. He knew that if the Echo failed, it would be a big failure and he became prepared for it.

Of course, Bezos realizes that not every risk is going to work out this way. In fact, he has taken risks which did not work out. But he also states that no one should let fear or mistakes ruin their chances of taking more risks. In fact, Bezos follows the belief that entrepreneurs should have to take risks and he isn't the only person to believe this. In fact, it's become a major topic in the business world today.

Taking risks won't be easy, and Bezos often discusses this fact. He knows that taking risks, especially in the beginning is scary and often concerning. However, it is important to start taking risks early and continuing this factor throughout your company's lifespan. If you are reading this biography to learn about how to take and handle risks, like Bezos does with Amazon, there are a few things you should keep in mind.

First, like Bezos has so many times, you are automatically going to imagine the worst. This is exactly what Bezos did when he started his online bookstore, he imagined it would fail. He has also done this with other risks within his company. It's a human trait which we all possess but it isn't necessarily a bad trait. Imagining the worst can help you prepare for it happening. It can help "soften" the disappointment as you can mentally prepare yourself for handling a disaster. It's also important to remember that we usually exaggerate what we imagine. We exaggerate how bad our risk will fail and the consequences of this. It is important to keep this in mind so you can be aware that, if your risk does fail, it probably won't be as bad as you imagine it to be.

Second, there are different types of risks. Of course, there are big and small risks, but there are also risks where you can calculate the success or failure. This is often the type of risk that Bezos likes to focus on because his team can measure what happens. In fact, they often won't use an idea that they can't measure, or they will try to find a way that they can measure the idea.

Another major type of risk that Bezos often takes is known as ambiguous risk. This risk is when you know some information, but you don't know everything. These are popular risks when it comes to business because the known information can help people understand where the risk sits in their business as a whole. No one ever wants to take a big enough risk that its failure could destroy the business. Therefore, it's often important to business people to know where the risk could fall on a scale.

Third, if you aren't willing to take risks, you shouldn't get into business. Bezos is a strong believer in this as he states business and taking risks go hand in hand. You cannot have one without the other. Bezos often looks at taking risks in this way: no matter what decision you make, you are taking some type of risk. For example, he could hire someone who is going to put in their two weeks' notice within the first couple of months. Risks are everywhere when you are building a business. In fact, there are sometimes so many risks that people don't even realize a certain decision might have risks involved.

Fourth, if you take risks, you are going to stand out from the crowd. As I have stated before, taking risks is scary which means a lot of people tend to shy away from risk-taking. Therefore, when people do start to take risks, they start to stand out in the business world. This often gets them and their business noticed, which can help bring in money and lead the company on the path to success. Even if your risk becomes a failure, this doesn't mean that people will remember you for the risk. It means that people will remember what qualities you have, which can bring you more opportunities in your career.

One of the biggest points that Bezos discusses in his interviews and presentations is that you can learn from your failures. You can learn what your customers don't want, or you can learn which ideas work and which ideas don't work. Bezos stresses that this is important because it is one of the ways that will help your company grow.

6. You Have to Think Long-Term

Bezos believes that one of the biggest mistakes many businesses do is that they get stuck in short-term thinking. He says that while thinking in the short-term is important, you also want to make sure that you're thinking in the long-term as both will help your company succeed. However, if you get stuck in one and don't include the other, the chances of your company failing increase.

For Bezos, the success of Amazon just happened. He was not expecting the success, especially at the rate it happened. By 2000, Amazon had beat out all of its e-commerce competitors, even though this was never on the mind of Bezos and the Amazon team as they don't worry about competition.

When it comes to measuring an idea, Bezos looks at the short-term and long-term effect the idea will have on the company. The proof that this type of thinking works is in Amazon's history. While the company started as an online book store, within a few years, Bezos included music and movies. This made the company's sales jump hundreds of thousands of dollars. A few years after that, Amazon started selling clothes, toys, electronics, household items, allowing third-party sellers, and so much more. This made Amazon's sales jump into the billions. Before Bezos agreed to start selling all these items, he looked at how the sales would affect the company in the short-term and the long-term.

Of course, this does not mean that Bezos and Amazon haven't had their struggles. Recently, Amazon has been testing a grocery service, which is known as Amazon Fresh. Fresh is part of Prime, therefore, customers should be able to receive their groceries within two days. However, when Amazon first started testing this service around several years ago many customers started having complaints. They complained that they had received spoiled food or that the service took longer than two days. People stated that the Amazon Fresh service made them question Amazon's ability as a whole. They no longer believed that Amazon Prime would give them their order within a couple of days, as promised. They then started asking why they should pay the $79 a year for Amazon Prime when their order is delayed.

For Bezos, he had been looking into a grocery service for Amazon since 2007. Ten years later, and he was getting various feedback about the Amazon Fresh service that would help him better the service. Like he had done with previous negative feedback, he welcomed it as it helped him find different avenues within Amazon Fresh that would make

Amazon customers happy. If you look at the history of Amazon Fresh today, you will see the changes that Bezos has made since launching the service. Furthermore, you will notice that with the changes, more customers started to feel happy with the service they received.

As Bezos believes, with every step and the feedback received on each service, you should take it and see how what you are doing now with your service will affect your company in the long-term. When Bezos noted negative feedback, he knew that he needed to get together with his team so they could find a solution to the problems they were facing within the Amazon Fresh service.

Amazon Fresh is a perfect short-term and long-term example because Bezos knew that the service would be an asset for the company, in the long-term. However, he also knew that the service would struggle in the short-term because there would be some factors that his team would have to fix in order to better the grocery service. Any business or entrepreneur can look at the history of Amazon Fresh and see how it's an example of how you know your long-term goals and continue to work towards them.

7. Marketing Strategies Can Change

Earlier I discussed how Amazon tried running ads through television stations and realized it wasn't worth the cost. For a few years after that, Bezos didn't think too much about marketing ads for Amazon and focused more on word of mouth. He believed that Amazon's best marketing strategy was the way people talked to others about Amazon. However, over the last year, more ads for Amazon have been seen in various places. This is because within the last couple of years Bezos has changed his thoughts on marketing. Even though he used to dislike the system of running ads for a company, he has now grown to like the idea and started advertising for Amazon.

One of the reasons Bezos says he had a change of heart over advertising is because the numbers proved that advertising can work. To test the idea, Amazon decided to advertise some of its own products, such as the Amazon.com website and the Echo. Through measuring, Bezos realized that these advertisements helped Amazon's sales (especially for the Echo) jump by about 72% in the United States. This launched Amazon into fifth place in advertisers in the United States.

Because Bezos informed his Amazon team of his recent mind change towards advertising in a company meeting in November 2018, we can expect to see more advertisements and changes coming from Amazon in the future. As Bezos always says, the company has to continue to grow and he is always looking for new ideas.

8. You not only want to be Stubborn but Also Flexible and Realistic

"If you're not stubborn, you'll give up on experiments too soon. And if you're not flexible, you'll pound your head against the wall and you won't see a different solution to a problem you're trying to solve"[13]

Bezos has been able to keep Amazon at the top of its game for years. When asked how he does this, he states that one of the biggest ways is by making sure he remains not only stubborn but also realistic and flexible. Bezos states that not only himself but also his team have to be stubborn in order to stay on top. They have to want this and make sure they keep this their goal.

At the same time, Bezos realizes that they also have to be flexible and realistic about where their company is heading. For Bezos, the three characteristics need to be managed on a fine line. He says that Amazon would have never been able to hold their rank if his team had become inflexible and "given up" when they saw one of their products or services fail. He says it was their stubborn determination to succeed yet remain realistic that not everything will succeed and be flexible about why something succeeds as something else

---

[13] Morris, 2017.

fails. Without being realistic and flexible, the Amazon team would have never been able to form clear ideas on how to stay on top of their game.

9. Use Algorithms

When Bezos and his team measure ideas or results from one of their tests, they use different algorithms. These are sets of rules that you follow in order to perform mathematical calculations, usually through a computer. They tell the software in your computer what to do. When you get into business, you will find algorithms everywhere and you will use them for nearly everything. An example of an algorithm that Amazon uses functions through your searches. If you search for music, you will find advertisements off and on the Amazon site which focus on your musical searches.

These algorithms not only increase Amazon's traffic, but it allows them to advertise the products they have. Amazon has billions of products and services which makes it impossible to know everything they have. Of course, people know they have the basic categories such as books, clothes, jewelry, kitchenware, etc. but people don't know exactly what items Amazon has until they search.

From your searches, these formulas can give you suggestions for other items you might be interested in. For example, if you go on Amazon and search for the movie *Gone with the Wind* you're going to find other suggestions that are similar to that movie or see what other movies customers who purchased that movie bought. By doing this, Amazon can increase their sales.

One of the key factors in using algorithms is that you have to find the ones that work for your company. For instance, if you have a small company, you won't incorporate the algorithms that Amazon uses. You might decide to use formulas from other sites, such as Facebook which allows you to use their algorithms or create ones specific for your company. Of course, as your business expands you will want to change your algorithms. As Bezos states, you want to make sure that when your company expands, everything else grows with it.

10. Adapt to New Technology

Bezos is a strong believer in you have to be willing to adapt to new technology. As you have seen in the last couple of decades, technology changes and it changes fast. Being able to adapt to this can be easier for some people than others. However, Bezos also feels that if you want to make your business successful in today's market, you will make sure you go along with the changing technology.

This might mean that you educate yourself and your staff on technology. You might spend time going to classes where you can learn more about Microsoft Office software or you might go to workshops which teach you how to use some of the newest technology available. This might also mean that you will need to step out of your comfort zone. Some people tend to shy away from technology because they are afraid of what mistakes they will make. As Bezos believes, mistakes are good as they help you learn. In fact, he states that people typically learn better from mistakes than simply learning about the topic.

Of course, one of the ways Bezos believes anyone can adapt to the new technology is to create it yourself. Amazon is no stranger to keeping one step ahead of the rest of the world when it comes to new technology. On top of this, Bezos keeps up to date on everything happening outside of his company when it comes to technology. For example, if he finds out that Apple is coming out with a new product, Amazon will quickly follow with their own version of the product. When smartphones became a popular technological device, Bezos was quick to meet with his team and develop a web-based mobile app which allowed people to shop on Amazon quickly and easily. This is an example of how Bezos makes sure Amazon stays on top, even if the company didn't develop the device itself.

Overall, Bezos believes that you have to be adaptable to anything when it comes to business. In fact, he often discusses in his presentations that business leaders who are more adaptable to what is going on in the world tend to establish more successful businesses than people who aren't as adaptable. Of course, this is not always an easy skill for everyone. Some people struggle to adapt to their surroundings. If you find yourself to be one who struggles, here are some tips that can help you adapt easier.

1. You will want to welcome failure. This is something that Bezos discusses a lot when it comes to his businesses. He states that people should not be afraid to fail as it can help lead your business in the right direction. He also notes that when people struggle to adapt, they tend to be afraid of failure. Therefore, the more you get into the mindset that you can overcome failure and help your business thrive, the more adaptable you will become.

2. You need to define your goals and don't let your goals define you. Bezos states that he remains mindful of Amazon's goals and mission every day. However, he also states that you cannot let your business's mission and goals become overwhelming because then they are defining you. Instead, you need to focus more on what winning can do for your company and less on the consequences of losing.

3. Don't let your ego take over. Even though Bezos is one of the richest men in the world, he does not let his ego

define him. While he is confident in his abilities, realizes his potential, and isn't afraid to say that all businesses should follow Amazon's policies in order to become successful, he also isn't egotistical about his skills either. He is very open to the possibility that every idea he has can fail and that someone can create a company better than Amazon. These realizations help Bezos remain more grounded and give him the motivation to do the best he can.

11. Make People Feel they are the Only Ones in the Room

One of the ways Bezos has become so popular as a businessman is because he will try to make sure people feel that they are the only ones in the room. Even if he is in a room with several people, he can make you feel that he is giving all his attention to you. Many people believe that by doing this and taking the steps to give personal demonstrations, he has increased sales for Amazon. For example, when the Amazon Kindle Fire tablet was released, Bezos didn't take the time to spend large amounts of money on advertising, give a big presentation on the Kindle Fire, or give a large press conference. Instead, he invited about 24 journalists into his office. He took the time to not only give them a tour but also take them into a room and show them the Kindle Fire personally. This not only made the person feel special, but they were also amazed because they had just received a personal demonstration by one of the most iconic CEOs in modern history. Sometimes, as Bezos proves, the way to sell new products is to make people feel special.

12. Every Day is known as Day One

Bezos uses the theory that every day is day one of the company because anything after day one is seen as its peak and then its decline, ultimately leading to its death. Bezos uses this theory because he doesn't want people to feel like Amazon cannot go up from where they see it at now. He feels that in order to keep his team working it's hardest to put out the best they have to feel like they are still at the starting point, which is day one.

Bezos has used this theory since Amazon's early days. However, it became more important when Amazon started to receive a top spot in during the early 2000s. As Bezos shared in his shareholder letter in 2016, "Day 2 is stasis. Followed by irrelevance. Followed by excruciating, painful decline. Followed by death. And that is why it is always Day 1."[14] Therefore, whenever he is asked a question from his employees about when Amazon will reach its peak, he always responds with never as in Bezos' mind the Amazon empire

---

[14] Bezos, 2017.

wants to do whatever they can so they never reach day 2.

However, in order to stay on day 1, Bezos realizes that every member of his team will need to focus on a few tips. Therefore, he came up with a handful of helpful tips which he believes will allow his staff members to stay in the day 1 mindset.

First, they are always supposed to follow the number one rule of Amazon which is customers are first. This means that they do not focus on the competition surrounding Amazon as it is this competition that can make them reach day 2. If they focus on making sure all their customers remain happy with Amazon products, they will focus more on building the company to become the best it can be every day they work there.

Second, is to embrace external trends. In today's world of technology, artificial intelligence (AI) is becoming a common interest among Amazon's customers. While some tend to worry about what AI can do in the long-term, many people are embracing the idea of robots and Amazon is one of these companies. However, they are not just stopping with Alexa, their current AI voice. Instead, they are looking to see where else they can go with AI and other external trends.

Third, when you are making decisions you want to make them quickly. You can make high-quality decisions quickly and this is what companies do when they are on day 1. He further states that companies which reach day 2 generally slow down their decision-making process. Therefore, Bezos wants his leaders to think on their feet and not take a lot of time making their decision. In order to help his employees through this point, Bezos states that they should remember all decision can be reversed. The more you pay attention to the results of your decision, the faster you will be able to reverse the decision. For example, if you start to notice that some issues are not in alignment, you can find a way to fix this and continue on with your progress.

Finally, Bezos tells his team, especially his managers that they always have to focus on the results they are getting from their customers. This includes emails, surveys, customer comments, and anything else. They have to focus on both the negative and positive feedback as this will help them remain in the day 1 mindset as they are always trying to focus on giving their customers exactly what they need and want.

13. Don't Just Work Long and Hard but Also Work Smart

This is one of the business lessons that Bezos learned a few years after he started Amazon. While he always paid attention to the people he was hiring, he never thought of making sure to hire the smartest people out of the hiring pool in the beginning. This doesn't mean that the people Bezos hired at first were not smart, they were, but they weren't the type of intelligence that Bezos needed in order to make sure his company continued to grow. However, he now only hires people which he feels are not only the smartest for a certain area and company overall but will also work long and hard.

While some companies will allow their employees to work smart and hard or long and hard, when you are working at Amazon, you have to have all three of these features or you won't be working at Amazon. This often means that while the employees can take a weekend off, they won't take the whole weekend off or they will still be finding time to work in other ways. For example, they might be thinking of an idea they can bring to a Monday morning meeting or they might be calculating the results of one of their new products. Bezos expects that his employees will always give their best to the company, no matter what time or day it is. Working 70 to 80 hours a week is normal when you are working for Amazon.

Of course, this business lesson is one which Bezos is not only honest about but one that former Amazon employees often discuss. In fact, this was first brought to the public in 2015, when The New York Times exposed part of Amazon's work environment with mixed reviews. People who had worked with Bezos stated that while the job can be demanding and sometimes brutal, Bezos pushes people to limits that they never realized they had. He makes sure that people can not only see the great and many things they can accomplish within the company but that they can always take it one step farther. Then, they can take it ever farther than this step.

In a sense, because Bezos is always working to give his best, he expects the same out of his employees. He believes this should be a factor in everyone's company, while the company might be demanding at a different level, they should expect their employees to give their best at all times.

Furthermore, it is through these factors and hiring people that will put everything they can into their jobs that has created the world of Amazon today. Employees often tell people that they work alongside some of the smartest people they have ever met in their lives. On top of this, their co-workers put their greatest strengths into their work and have the best leadership qualities. Furthermore, the leaders in every department never let their team settle with a task and never let any of their team members feel that they can't accomplish a certain task. Many employees state that when you feel you can accomplish anything in front of you, sometimes even more than you can ever imagine, your confidence rises and you start to take on new and exciting challenges every day.

Of course, the downside to having such a long work week is that people can find themselves burnt out from their job quickly. While there are many Amazon employees who have been loyal for years, Bezos realizes that he needs to make sure employees not only remain loyal but that they also have the energy to fulfill their mission. Unfortunately, this means that Amazon also tends to have strict firing policies.

14. Empower Your Employees

While reading about how the work environment at Amazon can be demanding, it's also important to note that Bezos does whatever he can to make sure that all his leaders lift up their team. Bezos realizes that if you want people to remain loyal and give you their best, you have to make sure that they feel positively about the people they are working for and the company. Therefore, Bezos is big on giving his employees the steering wheel, whether they are a manager or an employee under the manager.

Bezos believes that if the employee feels she had a part in the success of Amazon, she will gain more energy and be ready to bring forth more ideas and bring the company into the future. This is a method that Bezos has had since Amazon's early days as he told his customers in his first annual letter than in 1998, he would continue to hire the best people to bring Amazon into the future.

15. Keep Your Company's Culture in

Mind at All Times

From the beginning of Amazon, Bezos has maintained a certain culture. While the culture has remained practically the same, he has also made sure it grew along with the company. When doing this, Bezos stresses the importance of not changing the culture but just making sure the culture thrives the best it can at that moment. When you do this, Bezos states you need to remember that you don't make sure you have the best principles to follow but you create principles that will not only bring out your best but the best in your team.

Bezos states that one of the ways Amazon did this was by taking the last couple of decades and finding the most like-minded individuals. First, he worked to find leaders who could be in charge of their own area within the company that think like he does. He found leaders who will put their best into the company and do not pay attention to how many hours of work they put in but rather the type of work they put into their job. They aren't afraid of trying something new and failing because this will just further bring their area in the right direction.

When Bezos put his time in finding the right leader, he made sure this person would further this effort into finding the right team for his area of the company. The leader spent time making sure that everyone else hired for his team was just as energetic and determined as himself. Just as Bezos as had when he hired the leader for the area.

From there, Bezos made sure that he and the managers of the areas made other employees feel like they were just as important as everyone else on the team. They worked together to make sure that all the employees would put forth their best effort and do everything they could in order to help build up Amazon and take the company soaring into the future.

16. Stay Away from Procrastination

Jeff Bezos will be one of the first people to tell you that procrastination isn't just about putting off the work you need to do- it's also about putting off your ideas. When discussing procrastination, Bezos often talks about his decision to officially leave his highly beneficial and comfortable job on Wall Street and start his own business knowing very little about what he was doing and having very little money in the bank. He states that the longer he waited to make the leap, the longer he procrastinated on his life's professional dream.

Bezos brings this lesson into the world of Amazon and makes sure his employees realize that if they have an idea and they don't act on it immediately they are procrastinating. Even if the employee isn't sure that the idea is a good one, not acting on it is still procrastination. It is not taking the time to make sure the idea will hold up or that it's good, it's procrastinating because you are unsure of what the result of your idea will be.

Amazon runs a very tight ship and is a company with high demand. The employees who work for Amazon are constantly busy and, therefore, Bezos states they don't have time to procrastinate on even the slightest idea.

17. Keep Your Prices Low

Many companies will raise their prices or tell people they sell things at low prices yet their prices are higher than average for that product. Amazon doesn't follow this code. Instead, Bezos states that the company not only focuses on low prices but they are honest about their low prices.

Many third-party sellers who began using Amazon as a selling point found this out themselves. If they had a product that became high in demand, the Amazon team took note of this and created their own version of the product that the third party member was selling. On top of this, Amazon made sure to sell it at a lower price.

Bezos also states that you don't want to raise the price of the product just because it became popular. In fact, this is when you want to make sure the product stays at a lower price. The reason for this is because the lower your prices are; the broader range your customers are going to be. If you make your prices low enough, you will have customers that can purchase the item whether they work a minimum wage job or they make $30 an hour. In fact, Bezos states, this is often the goal of Amazon when they are looking into prices.

Of course, making prices low can often mean that the company loses money, however, this is usually only short-term. Because the price is so low there are millions if not billions of people who are able to purchase that same product. Therefore, Amazon will eventually start to make money off of that product. Even if it takes a few months, Bezos states the wait is typically worth it.

18. Before You Expand You Must Adjust Your Business Plans

When you first start your business, you don't know how far it's going to go. Instead, you just work hard and continue to do your best so your business can become successful. However, it is important to remember that as you expand your business, you also need to make sure to adjust your business plans. Starting Amazon from scratch, Bezos knows about this factor of businesses well.

Bezos tells people that their business will for sure be a failure if they don't know the details of their business. He further emphasizes this point by stating that they have to know these details before they focus on expanding their business. Expanding your business is always a great feeling, however, in order to make it successful you have to make sure that you understand every little bit of your business or your expansion will ultimately end in disaster.

When Bezos started Amazon, he never focused on how much money he could make at first. In fact, he never really focused on making sure Amazon was making the best profits they could. Instead, Bezos grew Amazon slowly and steadily, which meant that it took about 6 years before the company really started seeing profits. This happened because, at the beginning, the plan for Amazon was to focus on its growth and then it would focus on its revenue. Because of this, many people didn't want to invest in Amazon on the stock market. Furthermore, Bezos also took the money that Amazon was making and put it more towards investing in the company than creating a profit from it.

With each stage of growth Amazon saw, Bezos focused on creating a new business plan. For example, when Bezos would introduce a new area of Amazon he would go through the other areas and see what needed to change within these areas before he officially added another area. He would look at factors such as how the area ran from the leader down to other employees. He would look at how sales were going in the area, how customer satisfaction was, etc. If he noticed that something was missing within that area, he would include it in the new business plan. Bezos continued to go through this process with every piece of Amazon before he expanded the company.

By focusing on this process, Bezos has found that he is always revisiting his business plan. While some business leaders might find themselves getting tired of constantly going through the same process in their business plan, Bezos has grown to love it. Not only does it mean that Amazon is continuing to expand, which means it is still in the day one philosophy, but it also means that Bezos is able to revisit his business plan often. This has its own benefits, such as making sure that Amazon is keeping up with its goal of reaching 100% customer satisfaction and checking in to make sure his employees are doing everything they are supposed to so the company runs smoothly.

Bezos also feels that changing his business plan each time he expands his company takes away the constant need to remind oneself to check the business plan. Bezos maintains that every company should make sure they are revisiting their business plan often, more than once a year. However, Bezos also knows how quickly CEOs and other business leaders can push aside going over their business plan because they start to feel that their company is doing well, therefore, their business plan is working. For Bezos, this is a trap that can lead many companies to start declining. Bezos' advice is to revisit your business plan monthly, even if you are not expanding.

19. You Need to Watch How Often You Reinvent the Wheel

While Bezos prides himself on being unique and coming up with new ideas, he also knows there is a balance between creating new ideas and already working with what is out there. For example, Bezos states that while Amazon doesn't focus on how their competitors are doing in comparison to Amazon, he does look at factors such as what new devices Amazon's competitors are selling that Amazon is not.

Bezos states that the downside to constantly creating new products is you will end up spending a lot of your time proving to your customers that your new products are worthwhile. However, if they see that you are taking time to come out with a product that other companies have and just made a few slight changes to it, then you are able to gain those same loyal customers without having to always prove your product is worth their time and money. In a sense, Bezos has caught on to the idea that if he lets his competitors come up with a device, they will find out what works and what doesn't with this device. Then, Amazon will go to their own creative table and create a similar device that doesn't have the problems in the first device. They will also add different factors to it that the previous company didn't think of that Bezos and his team feel their customers will love.

Bezos states that this method helps them in the long run because it saves them a lot of time and energy. He states that many people don't realize how long it can take to develop a device. In fact, there are many products and services Amazon has now which took the company years to develop from the idea to releasing the invention to the world.

Bezos states you can also use this factor when you are working on establishing your own business. For example, he tells young entrepreneurs that he feels they should look into Amazon's policies because they are policies which work when building a business. However, Bezos also believes that you want to watch how much you take from another business. He advises that people take an idea and make it their own – one which will fit into their business better. You never want to mimic one company from the first policy down to the last policy because you will quickly learn that this is no longer your business. In return, you could lose your passion when it comes to your own business.

20. Be willing to Do What You Tell Others to Do

There are many people in leadership positions in a company that won't allow themselves to do what other people are doing. There are several reasons for this and it often depends on the person or the company. Sometimes people in management professions won't do what their staff does because they hire their staff to do these projects. Other people state they won't do other tasks because it is beneath them while some state it is because the company won't allow them to. The company states that everyone has their job descriptions when they start and it's this description they should follow. However, Bezos and his management team do not follow this path. Instead, they are all willing to do what they tell other people they need to do.

Bezos feels that this is important because it brings a sense of teamwork to the company. Employees who are lower on the employment ladder will feel that they are more equal to their supervisors and the CEO of the company if they see that these people will do their work with them. Bezos states this often gives him motivation and he is proud of the fact that though he has never been trained for every position Amazon has, he can work in every position and he has no trouble doing this if he needs to. In fact, sometimes Bezos can be seen visiting certain areas and jumping in to help staff members. While this is often a surprise for many Amazon employees, it is also a welcome surprise and leaves the employees feeling that they are truly an important part of the Amazon empire, which is something Bezos wants for his employees.

Another reason that knowing every role within his company is an advantage for Bezos is because he then knows every detail of his company. This will come in handy not only when he is working on recreating his business plan but also running Amazon as a whole. Furthermore, by knowing each job, Bezos is able to see what strategies the company can implement in order to make the occupation easier or even lighter so the employees can take on other responsibilities when helping to expand the company. On top of this, it can give Bezos a sense of what type of work goes into the role and how long the work should take. This can help Bezos establish when an employee is doing his best or what he can be doing better.

To get a better scope on how many jobs Amazon has within the company that Bezos knows, here is a list of various categories for jobs.

- Systems, Quality, & Security Engineering, which focuses on building and maintaining systems that are going to support some of the largest databases in the world. This is the area where you would gather the information from customer comments to see where Amazon can better its customer rating.

- The Research Scientists are the ones who take someone's idea and measure it to see if it will benefit the company in the short-term or the long-term.

- The public policy team are the ones who work outside of Amazon in order to give the customers their best in every area. They help create policies, often working with governmental leaders to do so, and take these policies to other areas of the company where they will be incorporated once they are approved.

- Development and Leadership training is the team that establishes the classes, training tools, and programs that ensure everyone at the company has the best training experience.

- Fulfillment and Operations Management are the center of your Amazon shopping experience. They are in charge of their areas and making sure that their staff get your items shipped to you in a timely manner.

- Editorial, Writing, & Content Management is the team which creates all of Amazon's written content. On top of this, they make sure the content is correct and edited so the customer has the best written experience possible.

- The Customer Service team is considered to be the heart of Amazon because they are the team that heavily focuses on making the company's goal of 100% customer satisfaction.

- Amazon's business intelligence team is the area which reads all of the data. Bezos knows that there are people who understand the numbers in business and people that don't. Therefore, he created this team so not all of the managers need to focus on all the numbers within their area. Instead, they can focus on other tasks which are just as important.

- The Buying, Planning, & In-stock Management area are the ones who make sure that Amazon has the required items so they can be shipped to you in two days or less. They go through the stock in their area and make sure that there is enough, which can reach upwards to thousands of the same items.

- The administrative support team is noted to be the team which helps keeps Amazon running as smoothly as possible. This team does everything from answering the phones to helping visitors to organizing major public events.

- The Facilities, Maintenance, & Real Estate team is the area which makes sure all of Amazon's buildings are working well. They go to various locations to make sure that everything is getting fixed, the bills that need to be paid are getting paid, and all the locations are looking their best inside and outside.

- Of course, when you have such a huge business, you're going to need a legal team to make sure that everything from products to contracts are legally binding.

- There are tons of other areas such as Human Resources, Marketing and Public Relations, Machine Learning Science, and Solutions Architect.

Knowing that these aren't even all the jobs within Amazon, it is truly amazing that Bezos can do each and every one of these jobs. Furthermore, Bezos believes that if he can learn the hundreds of jobs within Amazon then every CEO in the business world should be able to do the same thing.

For many people, knowing that Bezos could jump in and do their position at any moment can be a powerful motivator to help keep employees doing their best. However, this shouldn't be because they are fearful of losing their jobs as, while Bezos can do their position, he shouldn't have to. Instead, it can make employees feel more motivated because if the CEO of the company has no problem doing the work they are doing, then they should be able to accomplish their responsibilities to their greatest abilities.

21. Make Sure You Don't Give Out Any Information Unless You Have to

When you are running a powerful company like Amazon, you have to make sure that you're keeping as much information as you can private. Of course, there isn't anything Bezos can do about any employees who leave and then go to the newspapers to sell their story about working with Jeff Bezos at Amazon. However, there is a lot of control he has over this within his company and he is adamant that no matter what size company you have, you make sure that no information leaves unless it has to.

It doesn't matter what the company is doing. Nothing is mentioned outside of Amazon's walls until an official statement is made. This includes everything from Kindle books to any other type of merchandise or service. For example, when Bezos announced the delivery drones service or the Echo Fridge, they were all mentioned suddenly and people talked about these services because they were shocked to hear about them.

However, some areas of information are more important to keep secret than others. For example, no one knows how many employees Amazon actually has in the Seattle, Washington location, which is their headquarters. Furthermore, there is a floor in the company's headquarters building which is known as Area 51. This is the Amazon Kindle floor and there is absolutely no information which leaves the doors of that floor. In fact, other employees who work in the same building don't know what is going on when it comes to Area 51. On top of this, no employee, unless they have specific instruction to do so can step foot on the floor of Area 51. This is known to be a very strict rule within Amazon's headquarters.

One of the reasons Bezos runs Amazon this way is because the less information which is leaked to the public, the less his competitors are going to know. This is often the opposite thought process to other CEOs in businesses. In fact, many businesses often share what they are working on because this means that they can get people interested in the new and upcoming product. Bezos does not share this same idea. Instead, he feels that it's best to keep everything as secret as possible and then be able to officially launch the product or service and shock the world with what your company just released.

In other words, Bezos has learned from what he considers mistakes that other companies have made. Bezos has mentioned that members of his team have learned about what Amazon's competitors are doing and, therefore, they were able to create the same type of product but make it better. Bezos realizes that by doing this, he has taken some customers and money from the hands of his competitors. While he doesn't care too much about this, he also doesn't want anyone doing the same thing to his company as in order to stay near the top, Amazon has to be considered one of the most innovative companies in the world. Therefore, by learning from his competitors, Bezos has created a system within his company that doesn't allow other companies to learn what Amazon is up to and take their up and coming device a step further.

Bezos is even careful of what information he shares when he writes his annual shareholder letter. While he wants to keep his shareholders up to date on the company's information, he also doesn't want to give them too much information since his shareholder letters are public and everyone can read them. Therefore, this information can easily make its way onto another company's creative table.

While many people find businesses that keep so much information secret a bit worrisome, many other people have found Bezos' strategy to be one of a kind and brilliant. In fact, the more people realize how secretive Amazon really is when it comes to what the company is working on, especially when some employees state that there are thousands of ideas stated within the business every day, the more other business leaders realize they should follow the same path.

22. Always Remember to Give Back

While we discuss Bezos' philanthropy in another chapter, this is also one of the business lessons that Bezos discusses. He believes that it is important to give back not only within your company and locally but also in the world. He also believes that you need to create your own strategy such as picking certain areas that you mainly want to contribute to. For Bezos, these areas are education, science, and medical research.

Bezos was raised to give back to others. While Bezos likes to maintain a quiet atmosphere with where he gives and how often, his parents have an organization called The Bezos

Family Foundation which is known to be a highly active organization within its area.

One of the reasons Bezos is quieter about his charity work is because he feels donating to a charity takes as much mathematical work and effort as starting up your own business. Just like he does for everything in his career, Bezos takes his time in deciding what charities he will donate too and how much money he will give. He has donated to a variety of places through his own money and through money from his Amazon stock. Some of the places he has donated to include museums and other educational centers. I will discuss more about Bezos' charity efforts in a later chapter.

23. When it comes to Data, it begins at the Top

Jeff Bezos has always had a mind for data and this interest only increased once he started Amazon. In fact, Bezos, his managers, and his data team love everything to do with data. They are always tracking and discussing different ways they can measure data. It doesn't matter if it's about a specific Amazon location, product, service, what the customers want, how much the customers are willing to spend, or what the customer's favorite movie is – it is all about data when it comes to Amazon.

However, the number one rule Bezos states when it comes to data is that it starts at the top – with him. If he isn't interested in the data, then the data isn't going to go anywhere and you're not going to spend your time on it. At the same time, if his executive team doesn't agree to spend time, effort, and money on the data then the data isn't going to go anywhere. You have to have the support of the people in the company's top positions in order to do anything with the data. The data team at Amazon will spend their time focusing on the numbers because Bezos knows how important data is when you're trying to expand your business; which Bezos is always working on doing.

Because Bezos is the top of the company, he sees all the different types of data that his team wants to explore – and he makes sure to look into every single piece. Bezos is a strong believer that even if he feels looking into a certain thing is not necessary at first or sounds strange, he will continue to dig deeper into why his team feels the need to record this data. Furthermore, Bezos states that he typically understands the reason why and approves the data to be recorded and analyzed.

Bezos often gives the example of members of his team going to him with the idea to sell some space on Amazon's homepage for advertising. Because of Bezos' beliefs in advertising at the time, he thought the idea was ridiculous, however, he took the time to hear what his employees had to say. He then took the time to think about why they wanted to do this and how much it could help the company overall. He then realized through his own research that this was a great idea and he allowed his team to go through with it.

24. Get Rid of Bottlenecks

When it comes to business, a bottleneck is when production is stalled. This can happen for various reasons, such as the workload arriving too quickly. When a bottleneck occurs, you can lose a lot of money in your business because it delays production, which means that products don't get out for sale at the time they are supposed to. At the same time, because employees need to focus on eliminating the bottleneck, they are not able to finish other work that needs to get done. In a nutshell, a bottleneck can be stressful and cause a lot of problems quickly within the workplace. When this happens, employees can get frustrated with another employee or their job as a whole, which can bring its own set of problems.

Worse, bottlenecks can negatively impact customer satisfaction which is especially important for Amazon. Amazon is a huge company which prides itself on being a customer-centered entity. Because of this, the company is often under a microscope with thousands of people from their customers to reporters. If Amazon doesn't deliver customer service at its best, people quickly hear about it. People tend to naturally be tougher on Amazon when it comes to their customer service because of the mission of the company. However, Bezos doesn't seem to mind this as it helps him remain in touch with how Amazon's customers are feeling. He is also quick to be able to submit his own personal apology when it's needed in order to bring back customers.

But, because of this, Amazon needs to make sure that they can eliminate all bottleneck issues as much as possible and when they do occur, make sure that they can fix the problem as soon as possible.

This is another benefit for Bezos as he understands every position in his company. Due to this, he is able to identify where bottlenecks are happening in his business and can work with his team to fix it as quickly as possible. One of the ways he identifies bottlenecks is by looking at customer reviews, reviewing the business plan, and by reviewing every area within his business.

While bottlenecks might not be eliminated from your business, as not even Amazon has been able to eliminate them, Bezos believes that you can do your best to eliminate them as much as possible. He believes that as long as you stay on top of your business and know what is going on throughout your whole business, you will be able to fix the issue of bottlenecks in a good timeframe. The faster you can fix the issue, the happier your customers will be as they will be able to receive their product in the timeframe you provided. Furthermore, by frequently analyzing every area of your business like Bezos does, you will be able to cut down on the number of bottlenecks that occur within your business. Even if you can't eliminate them, being able to decrease the number of them that occur will help you increase your business.

25. Realize that Sometimes Things Will Come to You Later

When some people look at Jeff Bezos as he was moving from Manhattan to Seattle to start up his company and look at the major CEO now, they often become surprised at how much Bezos has grown as a businessman. The Bezos of today would probably never just up and leave without a highly detailed business plan to start up a company. However, this is what people believe Bezos did as he headed west towards Seattle. While many people believe he created his business plan while heading to Seattle, other people are not completely sure. When it comes to Kaphan, he is not even completely sure about what Bezos did. Kaphan states that there were times when Bezos took his time and truly thought about things. He would make flow lists, look at pros and cons, and then do a lot of research before coming to a conclusion, such as he did when deciding to sell books when first starting his business. However, there were also times where Bezos would just take a leap of faith and figure out things as he needed to.

In many ways, when he first started Amazon, he took many leaps of faith and problem-solved as certain things came up. Part of this was because, as Bezos will admit, he wasn't sure exactly what would happen once he started his company. He was a young entrepreneur and while he had some experience in helping other people run their business, he had never run his own business with only two other people. While Kaphan joined the Bezos' in Seattle, MacKenzie would eventually start working at Amazon as an accountant.

This is why Bezos sometimes states that while you want to try to learn and have a grasp of as much as possible so you can create your business plan, he also knows that things work out without fully planning all the time. Over the years, Bezos has changed along with his company. Instead of being a young entrepreneur, he is a highly respected and very knowledgeable CEO of one of the biggest companies in the world.

26. Make Sure You Watch Major Trends

Bezos has spoken openly about the fact that members of his Amazon team will watch to see what the company's competitors are doing so they can start working on a similar device that they will improve to make superior to the competitor's product. On top of this, Bezos states there are other members of his company which focus on researching and watching the major trends of the world. This is their main job because Amazon needs to stay up to date on all the new and upcoming forms of technology so they can keep their customers interested in purchasing their version of the device and won't bother buying anyone else's version.

When discussing the need to make sure you watch all major trends, Bezos often discusses the research he performed on the World Wide Web as he worked at D.E. Shaw. He states that before Shaw told him to look into the internet, he had no idea that the browser had become so popular. He states he will never forget reading the 2,300% growth rate during his research as this is something people rarely see. In fact, this is probably one of the highest growth percentages in history. It doesn't happen very much but another service which grew nearly as rapidly as the internet was Twitter, a social media platform which reached 2,100%.

In fact, Bezos often states that it is because of his finding through the internet research that he started to pay attention to trends. It was at this moment he realized how helpful this can be for businesses, especially ones like Amazon. Not only because they depend on the online market, but also because Amazon has so many services available. Therefore, Bezos makes sure that his team follows every single trend that they can think of from books to artificial intelligence. Bezos believes it really doesn't matter what it is, what matters is that Amazon employees are aware of the trend and can keep up with the demands of the market.

27. Bring Delayed Gratification into Your Business Plan

Bezos is a strong believer when it comes to the fact that you don't have to have gratification immediately. In fact, when it comes to business, it is a good plan to realize that delayed gratification is best. Delayed gratification is when people are comfortable with waiting for a temptation. For example, you don't expect to receive a lot of money when you first start your business, in fact, you are fine with waiting years before you truly see a profit. When it came to profit, Amazon followed the technique of delayed gratification and they continue to believe that this is an important part of their business.

When discussing why delayed gratification is important in business, he stated in an interview, "If everything you do needs to work on a three-year time horizon, then you're competing against a lot of people. But if you're willing to invest on a seven-year time horizon, you're now competing against a fraction of those people, because very few companies are willing to do that."[15] Because competition is not something that Bezos believes his company needs to focus on, he is a strong believer in how delayed gratification has helped his company overall.

However, delayed gratification can help a person more than just having the patience to wait for the money to start building up. There are many benefits of delayed gratification, and as Bezos is already aware, these benefits can not only help the company but also the employees within the company - all the way from the CEO down to everyone else.

You Can Save Money

Saving money in your business and personal life is a huge advantage for any entrepreneur and delayed gratification can help people learn that they don't have to get money right away, and if they do, they don't have to spend it immediately. Because delayed gratification helps control our impulses, it will help control our spending, which is a huge benefit when you are first starting your business. In fact, even Bezos continues to know that his business needs to continue to build up its net worth if it wants to remain on top. Delayed gratification is one of the ways Bezos has been able to achieve

---

[15] Winston, n.d.

this for so many years.

Delayed Gratification Helps You Focus on Other Areas

Bezos has taken a lot of time to discuss through his presentations and interviews that it often takes years for an idea to become public. Furthermore, once the new product or service does become public, it can take years to make sure it's exactly what the customers want. Because of this, delayed gratification can be a helpful tool as you will never find yourself rushing through a product just so you can turn around and start selling it because you are excited for the product to hit the market.

Delayed gratification can help you achieve the patience you need in order to do your best, to take time on a product, and to make sure that it is as perfect as possible before you start selling it to your customers. After all, if you send out too many products which your customers feel are not worth their money, they could soon start turning away from your business. Therefore, it is extremely important to make sure you are able to handle having to wait when it comes to developing new products and services. Bezos has found that following delayed gratification has helped him and other Amazon employees in this way greatly.

On top of this, delayed gratification can help you enjoy your job more. Because you are not in a hurry to make sure everything is done. You're comfortable making sure that you take your time so you can ensure your job is done correctly, you are going to feel less stressed and more content in your work environment. As Bezos often states about people being able to feel and feed off of other people's emotions, this can make your whole work environment better. For instance, if you are happy, your co-workers are able to feel happier about their work too.

People Feel More Appreciative in Their Lives

Bezos is a believer in the fact that you shouldn't focus on balancing your work and private life. Instead, you need to find a way to make sure they come together and become one. Bezos has also learned that when you do this, it means that if you appreciate your professional life, you're going to appreciate your home life. Delayed gratification can also help in this area as it helps people feel more appreciative about their life overall.

Not only do you come to appreciate other people, which can definitely help you in customer service, but you also come to appreciate hard work and other factors in your life. You start to appreciate the steps you have to take in order to make sure that a job is well-done. Of course, there are many benefits in your work life which follow from your mindset to perform your job to the best of your abilities, especially when you are working in Amazon as Bezos expects every employee to give their best.

28. Always Make Sure You over Deliver

By now you know that Amazon is a customer-centered focused company, which means they believe that no matter what, their customers are number one. Bezos has felt this is the most important method of business since he founded the company in the mid-1990s. Nearly 25 years later, Bezos still makes sure every member of his company does whatever they can for their customers. Even though he has a Customer Service department, which was created to specifically focus on making sure customers receive the best service whether it is through email, over the phone, or within Amazon's policies, Bezos still spends a lot of his own time on Amazon's customers.

Not only does Bezos take time to read the emails he receives from customers but he also spends time making sure that customers are satisfied within every department. Of course, this is often different than most businesses as Amazon has more than 20 different departments. However, this doesn't matter to Bezos because, as he believes, if he isn't ready to make sure he gives his best to his customers, then his team won't work to give their best.

There is very little Amazon won't do for their customers. Not only do they have policies which include refunding any item of theirs which was damaged when the customer received the item (even if it left in perfect condition from Amazon's warehouse) but also taking time to listen to their customers. Bezos and other Amazon team members will receive hundreds of emails every day which hold ideas from customers. These ideas range from changes on the Amazon website to products they would like to see Amazon start selling to ideas on improving products and even developing new products.

When you are a customer at Amazon, you can feel heard and respected whether it is on the phone, through email, or other means. If you talk to any Amazon employee which deals with customer service on a daily basis, this is not always an easy task. However, employees are never allowed to let a customer hang up the phone while they are still angry or to change their tone and become irritated with the customer. Amazon employees are always told to go above and beyond for the customer because, as Bezos often states, it is the customer that buys Amazon products. Therefore, it is the customer that can decide to turn away from Amazon. Furthermore, the customer can turn to thousands of other people online and tell them to stop shopping at Amazon for specific reasons. Bezos knows that this can bring his company down. Because of this, it is always best to give the customer the best service at all times.

However, going above and beyond means more than just giving the customer your best service. It means that sometimes an Amazon employee might give away free items in order to please a customer. This can also mean that Amazon decides to try out one of the customer's ideas, even if this idea will cost the company a bit of money. After all, if Amazon employees can bring ideas to the table and cost the company money as they test these ideas as products, customers can also do the same.

Of course, because Amazon is an online store, this means that customer service is typically done online through email or surveys. For many people, this is a different type of customer service, one which they believe is often easier than if you are face to face with a customer. But, at the same time, Bezos states that this is also where the business world is heading in the future. Amazon has worked on perfecting above and beyond customer service online, and if you talk to millions of people all around the world, they believe that Amazon has done a great job perfecting this online service.

29. Always Use the Two Pizza Rule

Bezos realizes that many companies struggle with having to balance creativity and productivity at the same time. Of course, this has been a struggle for Amazon from time to time, especially in the company's early days. However, Bezos has stated that there is a simple way to do this by using what they call the two pizza rule.

The trick of the two pizza rule is really very simple and is exactly how it sounds. The rule goes like this: if it takes more than two pizzas to feed a team, then the team is too big. However, this doesn't mean that you let go of people. Instead, it means that you make two teams out of the one large team.

Bezos states that it is important that people work in smaller groups and it helps keep everyone productive and creative. He states that when some people are placed in large groups, they start to become more reserved or quiet. Some people also can't think productively in a large group. Because of this, and the fact that thousands of people work at Amazon throughout the world, Bezos is a big follower of this rule. In every team, they can all be fed through ordering two pizzas.

Bezos isn't the only businessman who feels that smaller teams are better to have throughout the company. In fact, there are many companies that tend to make sure they keep smaller teams over larger ones. On top of this, there are many professionals outside of the entrepreneur world that believe the same thing.

After Bezos' two pizza rule became public, many people started researching how well smaller groups work over larger groups. Below are several benefits which you can think of as you are working towards your own company.

Social Loafing

Social loafing is a term which became popular during the 1970s. Alan Ingham created the term when he was trying to explain one of the downfalls of larger teams over smaller teams. He stated that social loafing happens when individuals decide that because there are so many people which are part of their team, they don't have to put in as much effort into the team's work as other people. Social loafing is, unfortunately, easy for people to do and even some of the smartest people can be caught being a social loafer. In fact, if you think back to your school days, or when you are in groups in your class, you might find that you are sometimes a social loafer or one of your other group mates can be one at times.

It isn't that social loafing is a negative term, it is simply the fact that when people start becoming social loafers, then the whole group can suffer. Sometimes people get frustrated by people who are social loafing and other times when one person in the team starts to do less work, then other members of the team start to follow this direction. There are many downfalls of social loafing, and it is believed to be a natural human reaction for most people. Therefore, Bezos states, it is just best to avoid large groups completely as then there will be less social loafers if the group is smaller.

It is important to remember that social loafing is different from The Ringelmann Effect, which I will discuss a bit later. With social loafing, members often feel that they are not heard or won't be heard because of all their other team members. Therefore, it's not really that they don't want to participate, it is simply because they start to feel pushed aside or that other members have better ideas than they do. On top of this, some people suffer from psychological disorders, such as social anxiety, which is when they start to get anxious around a lot of people and will be less able to contribute.

Engagement

Bezos is one that reads up on as many studies and features as he can. This includes anything he is thinking about changing in the workplace. He wants to make sure that anything he changes will affect the company and the customers as a whole positively. Therefore, another reason Bezos started to believe strongly in the fact that keeping groups small within Amazon was necessary was through all the studies conducted in businesses throughout the United States showing that small teams are more engaged than larger teams.

In fact, according to one study, if there were less than ten members on each team, engagement within the groups went up 42%. When this study compared these findings to corporations which had larger groups, the results showed that only about 30% of the employees in these companies were engaged. For Bezos, this 12% is enough to make sure he and his departmental leaders do everything they can in order to keep smaller groups within Amazon.

The Ringelmann Effect

As stated before, the Ringelmann Effect is different from social loafing, even though the terms are often used interchangeably and confused. The biggest difference to remember is that social loafers are not trying to take the easy road because they are in a large group, they literally feel that they do not have as much to give as other group members. However, when people use the Ringelmann Effect, they purposely decide to take the easy road because they feel that there are other people who can do the job for them.

Maximilien Ringelmann, a French professor, established this concept after he asked a group of his students to play a game of tug-o-war. While his students played, Ringelmann watched and noticed that the more students he added on each side, the more students would start to put less effort into their work. It wasn't because they began to run out of room or couldn't pull the rope with so many people on their side. It was simply because they felt that because there were so many other people, they didn't have to work as hard.

Bezos is not the type of CEO who will take less effort from any of his team members. Because each employee is supposed to want the best for the company, and Bezos himself works incredibly hard to make sure the company runs smoothly, he demands the same from his staff. Therefore, Bezos is going to do whatever he can to make sure he doesn't create an environment which will allow some of his employees to put less effort into their work. This is why Bezos maintains the two pizza rule at Amazon. Not only is it a fun time when his teams are able to take a break from their hectic days and have pizza as a team, but it will also help the managers make sure that their teams aren't getting too large.

30. You Don't Have to Communicate

Jeff Bezos surprised everyone at a business retreat he was at when they talked about how people should always communicate in a company. Instead of agreeing with everyone else, Bezos stood up and yelled that people should not be communicating because this is a sign of a bad business. Other business people who were there stated everyone just turned to look at who yelled this, and it happened to be one of the most popular CEOs of modern history.

But why would someone who is so tight on customer service, which is constant communication, and small teams feel that communicating is bad? The answer to this is simple, according to Bezos, it means that your teams are too big. He states that if your teams are small enough, there is no need to communicate because everyone knows how to work together to keep the company running like a well-oiled machine.

Furthermore, Bezos states that communication is bad because then it means that the system is too organized. At Amazon, people know who the CEO is and they know who their supervisors are. They know who their co-workers are, specifically in their own teams. They know what people's roles are around them, but this doesn't mean that there is a strict order inside the walls of Amazon. In fact, Bezos would rather have a lack of communication because this means that the system is disorganized and anyone thinks they can come up to the CEO with their idea - which is exactly what Bezos wants.

31. Never Let Someone Steer You Away From Your Vision

By now, you realize that Jeff Bezos is big on ideas, passionate, and strong in his vision. After all, if he didn't believe in all three of these things then Amazon might not exist. However, Bezos doesn't just believe that he should be the one to follow his dreams, he thinks that everyone should be able to follow their dreams. Above all, Bezos believes that no one should ever let anyone steer them away from their vision, no matter what happens.

There are many business lessons that I discussed in this book that Bezos strongly believes in. However, this is one of the most important when it comes to Bezos. In fact, many people feel his passion to make sure other people believe in themselves and follow their dreams ranks up there on his list close to customer service.

Even though former Amazon employees have been noted to say that Bezos runs a bit of a tight and demanding company at Amazon, he is also one of the first people that employees can feel a sense of support from. While his advice and support might come off as a bit strong to people, it's really just the way Bezos communicates. Many employees state that he is naturally an intense guy and full of energy. On top of this, he is very passionate about everything he believes. When he is so passionate, he tends to put everything he has into what he is doing and saying. Therefore, people feel that he can come off as difficult to work with or even tough. However, many other employees state when you start to see around the tough exterior you see a guy who just wants the best for everyone in his company. You see a guy who strongly wants the best for his customers and is trying everything he can to make all this happen. You see a guy that wants to see people succeed in their visions.

In the same guy, is a man who was told that his online world's largest bookstore idea would not work out. In fact, when Bezos was talking to people about first starting his company, people either liked or didn't like the idea. And, as Bezos will tell his audience, there were a lot more people who didn't like the idea. However, he did not let this steer him from his vision as he knew in his gut, it would work out. While he didn't know how big Amazon would become, he did know that it could reach a wide range of people. And he was right. Everyone who said that he shouldn't go through with his idea was wrong. Bezos himself often asks people to think of a world without Amazon. What would have happened if Bezos had listened to all the people who told him not to follow his vision?

Therefore, Bezos is a true believer in no matter who or how many people tell you not to follow your vision or to pick another career path, you need to continue on the path you are on. Bezos states that you have to find what you are passionate about and work towards that vision.

32. Set the Biggest Goals You Can Dream Up

There are people in this world, and Jeff Bezos is one of them, that believe if you imagine it happening it will come true. Therefore, one of Bezos' key business lessons for success is that if you reach for the biggest goals you can set for yourself and your company, if you take the time to imagine yourself reaching these goals, they will come true. Bezos also states that if you continue to remain determined and work hard, you will reach your goals.

However, he also states that it is important to make sure you never stop giving yourself new goals to accomplish. Even in Amazon, a multimillion dollar company which has been at the top for years still has goals that they are trying to reach. This is because Bezos and his team are always finding new goals for the company, especially once they reach a previous goal.

Bezos believes that making sure you put a new goal in place of the goal you just reached is just as important as making sure you take time to celebrate hitting your goal. In order to keep your own mental state and morale towards the company healthy as well as that of your employees, you also need to take time to celebrate your goals, big and small, with your staff and everything done inside your company is really a team effort.

However, Bezos also states that you need to remain realistic with your goals. He doesn't like goals which are thought to be overly optimistic. While he wants people to reach beyond their wildest dreams, he also wants people to stop and think about their work, what their business is about, and make sure that this goal is going to fit in the mission and vision of their company. If it isn't or if you find that this goal might be overly optimistic or unrealistic, just scale it down a bit.

33. Make Sure You Have a Team of Top Achievers

I have already discussed the demanding culture that many former employees state Bezos creates at Amazon. However, when you create a company like Bezos, one which is full of people who not only focus on achieving their goals but go above and beyond, you become demanding because you know what your employees can do. Furthermore, you often become demanding because you need to be in order to keep up with the demands of your company, which is exactly where Bezos sits with Amazon.

Since the beginning of Amazon, Bezos worked hard to create a strong team. However, in order to create the team that Amazon needs today, he needs to make sure that the people he works closest to, such as his lead managers and other staff, are some of the hardest workers and aren't afraid to put in more than they thought they could because they are strong achievers.

Bezos states that in order for him and his hiring team to make sure they are hiring the right people, they not only focus on a hiring bar, which is something that I have discussed previously, but Bezos also likes to meet them to ask them a variety of questions. He might ask more history career type questions or he might simply ask if they look for a life and work balance. On top of this, Bezos makes sure that some of his top employees, the ones he depends on to make sure that things are running smoothly within the smaller groups, have degrees, achieved high milestones in their college years, and even got high scores on their ACT or SAT tests. Bezos isn't afraid to ask any question that he legally can in order to make sure he is hiring the best top achievers for his company.

34. Don't Become too Obsessed With the Stock Market Prices

Today, most companies get a stock that investors can buy and sell in the stock market. Amazon did this about two decades ago when Bezos started to sell shares for $18 each. Today, Amazon's stocks are worth much more and continue to grow. However, there are also times when their stock prices have been known to fall. When it comes to this, Bezos never worries and he doesn't want any other business owner spending time worrying about their stock price either.

Bezos states that one of the key features of stocks is that the prices naturally go up and down. Usually, these numbers don't mean anything. Before getting into the stock market, whether it is because you're going to get your company a share or because you want to invest in the stock market, you need to understand the basics. One of these basics as not only Bezos talks about but also Warren Buffett, who is one of the greatest investors in modern history, is that the reason the price of stocks increase or decrease is because people are buying or selling the stock.

When people buy the stock, the price of the stock increases. However, when people sell the stock the price decreases. Just because there is a bit of decrease doesn't mean you should run off and sell your stock. Let it sit as, chances are, the stock will increase and you will be making even more money off your investment later.

Furthermore, an investing business lesson that Bezos has learned over time is one he commonly shares when he discusses stocks and this is you want to pick a stock that you will want to hold for a long time. In fact, your ultimate goal should be that you want to hold the stock forever. This is often not a huge method with many investors. They often will sell a stock when it gets to a certain amount, whether high or low in price, in order to make money or try to save as much money as possible. However, Bezos states that if you used the buy and hold method, which is when you don't plan on ever selling or trading your stock, you are going to make more money in your investments. Of course, this can further the profits of your company.

35. Don't Strive to be Perfect, Strive to Do Your Best

Bezos has stated that when people work as hard as his employees do in their jobs, they often become overly critical of themselves and will start to overthink because they believe everything they do has to be perfect. However, Bezos states this is the wrong way to look at it. Instead of thinking you have to be perfect, which isn't humanly possible, you just have to focus on doing your best. This is all he asks from his employees, that they work hard and do their best.

Bezos hires the best people for his company, he knows what top achievers look like and when he finds one, he snatches them up as quickly as possible. Because of this, he knows what they are capable of, even if they often don't. Since he knows that they are capable of more than they ever let on, he often pushes them to do their best, which they believe is more than they can handle. However, for the employees that stick around, they soon find that Bezos was right. He believed that they could accomplish more than they previously thought and they did.

However, Bezos also believes that once you realize you can achieve more - you need to work harder in order to achieve even more. It is just like setting goals for your own area, when you reach one goal, then you set another goal which is higher than the previous goal. This doesn't mean that you are striving to be perfect or that Bezos believes you can reach perfection. It means that Bezos has faith that you can take on more than what you give yourself credit for.

36. Always Question everything you are Going to Do - But only to a Point

While there are many other business lessons that Bezos often discusses, the last one I will talk about in this book is that you always want to question everything before you do it but, at the same time, you don't want to question it too much.

Bezos believes there is a fine line in nearly everything that you do. While you want to make sure that the idea you come up with for your business is going to help your business, either short-term or long-term, instead of hurt your business, you also don't want to spend too much time thinking about the pros and cons of your idea as this is overthinking. Instead, ask yourself a few basic questions, such as "Is this something that the customers are going to want?" or "How much will this cost the company in the short and long-term?"

Whenever Bezos hears of a new idea, he is always asking himself several questions about the idea, however, he won't spend a lot of time on it either. He will ask himself a question, think of the answer, and then move on to the next question or simply decide if he no longer needs to spend time on the idea.

Chapter 10: Philanthropy

When it comes to giving back, Bezos believes that this goes beyond his community. In fact, the whole Bezos family has taken part in giving back to as many people as they can all around the world. In order to fund his philanthropic efforts, Bezos uses the money he receives from Bezos Expeditions. While Bezos has been reported to fund several projects and donate to countless charities, he remains quiet in his philanthropic efforts. Because of this, some people are not sure of all the projects and charities Bezos supports, however, they do know that he likes to give back.

Many people feel that compared to what Bezos was worth, he put very little effort into charities until he became known as one of the richest men in modern history. However, other people state that just because there is little report of his charity work, doesn't mean he didn't give to nonprofits or help support other missions.

In 2017, Bezos went to his Twitter to ask his supporters what type of charity work they thought he should get involved in. Bezos wanted to figure out a strategy that he could use to give back to the people who deserve it the most in the United States. He felt that reaching out to his supporters on a social media platform would allow him to get the best sense of the areas where philanthropic effort is needed the most. His followers quickly replied, but it took about a year for Bezos to announce his decision.

After going through the feedback from his followers, Bezos stated that he was going to focus on educational programming in underserved communities. On top of this, he also stated that he was going to go into these same communities and figure out a strategy on how he can help the homeless population. This was the first time that Bezos ever went public with his philanthropic efforts.

The Bezos Day One Fund

Bezos continued his announcement by stating that he decided to put $2 billion dollars into educational programming and housing for the homeless. He stated that this short-term strategy is known as The Bezos Day One Fund. The name of the fund comes from Bezos' own daily strategy, which he calls the "day one" strategy. He states that he strives to maintain this mindset as it is the mindset which has helped him achieve his goals throughout his career.

There are two parts which make up the Bezos Day One Fund. The first part is the Day One Academies Fund, which focuses on education, and the second part is the Day One Families Fund, which focuses on supporting homeless families. Bezos named his former Amazon teammate, Mike George, as president of the organization. George worked with Bezos on

Amazon products such as the Echo and Alexa.

The mission for the Day One Academies Fund is to develop new tier-one preschools for low-income families in the selected underserved communities. However, these preschools will not be just any type of preschool. They are to be the best preschools that the fund can support. They are to be high-quality preschools which offer a full scholarship for families. They are going to follow the Montessori preschools progress and curriculum. A Montessori preschool is a type of school which has a very progressive curriculum. At the same time, children who attend these schools are encouraged to make their own decisions. The goal of the teacher is to then help guide the students, so they can learn where their decision will take them.

Another large part of the Montessori-based educational program is the number of activities the children take a part in. The schools don't tend to run in a typical way, where the teacher is in front of the class and teaching the students throughout the school day. Instead, the children are in a room where they are encouraged to work together, which helps them learn the value of teamwork. On top of this, there are usually different ages in the school, which allows children to learn how to work with kids who are older and younger than them. Together, they help each other work towards mastering the life skills they will need outside of the classroom walls.

The aim of much of the curriculum is to teach the children how to take care of themselves. The Montessori style school was established by Maria Montessori, an Italian physician, who didn't feel that the type of education students received in the early 1900s was very useful. Montessori felt that children learn better through natural life experiences. On top of this, if they learned this way, Montessori felt that they would be able to make the best decisions as adults and be able to lead successful lives.

This is also much of the aim for The Bezos Day One Academies Fund. Through the feedback and research which went into creating the Bezos Day One Fund charity, Bezos realized that one of the reasons people struggle with homelessness is because they were never taught the life skills they needed. While they received an education, sometimes a college education, the schools they attended did not focus on teaching them life skills. Therefore, when they went out into the world, they struggled financially, which often meant that they were unable to afford a place to live. Furthermore, Bezos looked closely into the curriculum in the majority of schools and found that students are often bored or falling behind. He found that teachers are often too busy with the other students, grading, or other responsibilities and they can't focus on the children who need them the most.

Through his research, Bezos realized that the Montessori style school would be the best way to help children in underserved communities. Not only would they be able to attain a better education, but they would be able to learn the life skills needed to succeed. Within the Day One Academies Fund, Bezos uses the same principles as Amazon. He sees this as a "testing point" and feels that if his team continues to measure the success of the Day One school that they might be able to take this effort farther in the future.

The Day One Families Fund focuses on homeless families in need of support by helping the many nonprofits which focus on homelessness. Not only do these charities focus on finding shelter for the families, but they help the families get back on their feet. They make sure the families are fed, the children receive an education, and some charities even help the parents find a job. The mission of the Day One Families Fund is that no child sleeps outside.

Starting in 2018, this fund has been giving to various charities through an annual leadership awards program. The fund awarded 24 organizations with awards ranging from $2.5 million to $5 million. In total, the Day One Families Fund gave out $97.5 million. Altogether, the Day One Families Fund supported organizations in 16 states and the District of Columbia. The recipients and their amounts were as follows:

1. Abode Services located in Fremont, California, was awarded $5 million.

2. Catholic Charities Archdiocese of New Orleans located in New Orleans, Louisiana was awarded $5 million.

3. Catholic Charities of the Archdiocese of Miami located in Miami, Florida, was awarded $5 million.

4. Catholic Community Services of Western Washington located in Tacoma, Washington, received $5 million.

5. Community of Hope which is located in Washington, DC received $5 million.

6. Community Rebuilders located in Grand Rapids, Michigan, received $5 million.

7. Crossroads Rhode Island, which is located in Providence was awarded $5 million.

8. District Alliance for Safe Housing or DASH located in Washington, DC received $2.5 million.

9. Emerald Development and Economic Network located in Cleveland, Ohio, received $2.5 million.

10. FrontLine Service which is also located in Cleveland, Ohio, received $2.5 million.

11. Hamilton Families from San Francisco, California, was awarded $2.5 million.

12. Heartland Family Service which is based in Omaha,

Nebraska, received $5 million.

13. Housing Families First located in Henrico, Virginia was awarded $2.5 million.

14. JOIN based in Portland, Oregon received $5 million.

15. The LA Family Housing from North Hollywood in California received $5 million.

16. Northern Virginia Family Service located in Oakton, Virginia, received $2.5 million.

17. Primo Center for Women and Children which is based in Chicago, Illinois, received $2.5 million.

18. Refugee Women's Alliance in Seattle, Washington received $2.5 million.

19. The SEARCH Homeless Services from Houston, Texas received $5 million.

20. Simpson Housing Services in Minneapolis, Minnesota received $2.5 million.

21. The Salvation Army's Center of Hope located in Charlotte, North Carolina received $5 million.

22. The Salvation Army of Greater Houston in Texas received $5 million.

23. UMOM New Day Centers from Phoenix, Arizona,

received $5 million.

24. The Urban Resource Institute in New York City received $5 million.

Every year, the updated recipients of The Day One Families Fund will be announced on the Day One Fund website.[16]

Other Charities

For the last few years, Bezos has been noted as giving to various charities and funds, including retrieving the F-1 engine which sat at the bottom of the Atlantic Ocean. After the F-1 engine was uncovered, Bezos decided to donate the item to the Seattle Museum of Flight.

Starting around 2009, Bezos started supporting the Fred Hutchinson Cancer Research Center. The last time it was noted he donated here was in 2017. In 2013, Bezos received word that one his former Amazon teammates founded his own charity known as Worldreader. In support, Bezos donated about $500,000. In Seattle, Bezos has donated several thousand dollars to projects for the Seattle Museum of History and Industry, including funding their innovation center.

---

[16] "The Bezos Day One Fund", n.d.

In 2017, Bezos decided to donate $1 million to the Reporters Committee for Freedom of the Press organization, which provides services to American journalists who have found themselves in legal trouble with their articles. The following year, Bezos focused on The Dream Fund, which helps undocumented immigrants receive a college education. These immigrants were brought into the United States as minors and now, as adults, they are trying to remain in the United States and receive a college education. That same year, Bezos started focusing on supporting veterans, specifically those who are interested in running for political office. This organization is known as With Honor, and its mission is to provide help to veterans who want to help other veterans through running for governmental offices.

Chapter 11: Politics

Many people feel that one reason Bezos' Amazon Company took off like it did was because he didn't have any type of political motives for the company. On top of this, Bezos has kept politics out of his businesses, which isn't a common practice for successful businessmen at Bezos' level. This is often what makes Bezos a bit different from many other top businessmen. However, this doesn't mean that Bezos has not discussed politics. In fact, his political discussions have become more common over the last couple of years. However, this is not just because of comments Bezos has made.

Through his public campaign finance records, Bezos tends to vote Democrat. For example, he supported Maria Cantwell and Patty Murray, both Democratic Senators. On top of this, Bezos tends to support politicians who aim to provide better technology in the future. For example, he has shown support for representatives such as Spencer Abraham and John Conyers who focus on internet issues. Bezos has also donated to PAC, Amazon's political action committee, which has supported both major political parties over the years.

While he does so quietly, Bezos is known to support many political social causes, such as same-sex marriage. In fact, not only has he supported the legalization of same-sex marriage, but he also donated $2.5 million to the Washington United for Marriage group.

Much of Bezos' political stands came out when he bought The Washington Post. Before Bezos officially took over, the newspaper wrote an article where they discussed the new owner, focusing on what they could write about his political side. The article discusses that some people who know him state that he is a libertarian and has donated to charities in support of this cause. However, when it comes to voting, he typically stays Democratic, but he is supportive of both major political parties. The article also dives into the fact that many of Bezos' political beliefs stem from his mother and stepfather, who often supported measures which focused on creating a better world for children, such as better educational systems.

The most public political stance for Bezos occurred when he declined Donald Trump's offer to join his Defense Innovation Advisory Board in the 2016 Presidential Election. While Bezos never publicly spoke about his decision, mostly because he tries to maintain a private life, President Donald Trump has spoken publicly against Bezos multiple times since he declined the offer. Trump has often taken his thoughts to the social media platform, Twitter, where he accused Bezos of spreading "fake news" which undermined his presidency and avoided corporate taxes. The only comment that Bezos has ever made against Donald Trump was joking he would use one of Blue Origins' rockets in order to send the president into outer space.

Saudi Vision 2030

When it does come to Bezos becoming more public over politics, it is normally because it involves business. For example, in 2018, Bezos met with the de facto ruler and crown prince of Saudi Arabia, Mohammad bin Salman, in Seattle to discuss opportunities for what is now called Saudi Vision 2030.

The Saudi Vision 2030 is a vision for Saudi Arabia's future, which focuses on the strengths and capabilities that the country can reach. In this vision, Salman wanted to reach out to the founder and CEO of Amazon in order to discuss possible avenues of cooperation. The main reason for this was because part of the Saudi Vision 2030 is to bring more technology into Saudi Arabia. On top of this, Salman wants Amazon to open a data center in his country.

Chapter 12: What Motivates Jeff Bezos

No matter who you are, there is going to be something that motivates you. Whether you need to focus on a simple task, a larger task, or run one of the biggest businesses in the world you will need to have a source of motivation. Sometimes, finding your motivation to accomplish a task is easier than other times. Sometimes people start to feel like they are dragging and other times people feel like they can take on anything. Like the rest of us, Jeff Bezos has seen his good days and his bad days when it comes to his motivation. Of course, as in many other pieces of his professional life, he has shared the things that motivate him.

Why Motivation Matters?

Bezos will be the first person to tell anyone that motivation is a huge factor when it comes to success. Without motivation, you will not be able to find and hold the ambition you need in order to complete the tasks which will make you successful. According to science, motivation occurs because of the benefits it holds. This means that the more we feel the benefits of motivation, the more likely we are to feel motivated. Just as Bezos discusses the circle between your personal and professional life, there is a circle between motivation and its benefits.

Motivation Brings Rewards

Rewards are a big benefit of motivation. When we complete a task, we are often rewarded in many ways. For example, we can feel rewarded because the task is complete, because we accomplished a goal, and because we learned what we are capable of. Sometimes there are rewards in terms of money. For example, whenever someone makes a purchase on Amazon, Bezos' wealth increases. Because of this, he can feel more motivated to make sure his customers are happy so they will continue to purchase items from Amazon.

You Learn When You Are Motivated

By now you should realize that Bezos is continuously learning through his company. Furthermore, he also strives to make sure that his team continues to learn through their jobs, such as having to write out their weekly reports so they can critically think about the sales. Since his childhood, Bezos has found that he can learn from everything, whether it was a robot he created at the age of 10 or developing new Amazon services. He learns whether a device fails, such as the Amazon Fire Phone, or succeeds, such as Amazon Prime.

When he learns something, Bezos feels a sense of motivation to do better and move his company another step up. For example, when Amazon first launched Amazon Fresh, Bezos learned that there were factors, such as how to keep purchased food fresh, that the company needed to work out. Therefore, he took this as a learning experience to create a better grocery outlet within Amazon. This kept Bezos motivated towards his goal of including groceries. It also furthered his motivation to continue to try other ideas for the company.

Motivation Creates a Sense of Competition

I discussed how Bezos does not focus on competition of other retail stores earlier. However, this does not mean that there is never a sense of competition, it is just a different form of competition. Instead of focusing on other retail stores, Bezos focuses on his customers. He has created a sense of competition by always focusing on reaching 100% in customer satisfaction. This means that there is not one customer who is unhappy with a product bought from Amazon. For most people, this would seem impossible. However, because Bezos looks at this as a form of competition to always do better than the last time, he has a strong sense of motivation to achieve this goal.

Motivation Brings Curiosity

From the beginning, Bezos has been curious to see not only what he could accomplish in his life but also what Amazon can accomplish. Because Bezos is constantly working towards finding what works well, what doesn't work, and trying new things, he is motivated to continue working. He wants to know how far he can take things, but also feels that there really is no stopping point. Psychologists agree that this type of curiosity is a huge factor for motivation.

What Bezos Says Motivates Him

Through his presentations and interviews, Jeff Bezos has discussed the factors of his life that motivate him to continue doing the best job he can in and outside of his businesses. While I cannot discuss everything Bezos has stated in this book, I have included several of his comments. Bezos believes that in order to do your best, you need to find your motivation. It is important to remember that you can find motivation as you work towards your goal. Not only do you need to start with motivation, but you also need to continue to feel your motivation to so you can keep working towards your dreams.

Jeff Bezos is not like many other businessmen. Even though he has built the Amazon empire from scratch he still takes time to read emails from customers who have a complaint. He states that after reading these emails, he will then forward them to the appropriate staff member asking them about the complaint. Bezos doesn't do this because he wants to investigate the complaint, he does this because he wants the employee to fix it so the customer can be happy.

For many business owners at Bezos' level, this is not the type of work they accomplish during the day. Most CEOs with such a large business hire staff to deal with the day to day responsibilities, such as customer complaint emails. However, for Bezos, it is one way he stays motivated to make sure Amazon is running as smoothly as it can be.

But these emails aren't the only thing that keeps Bezos motivated. In fact, there are several factors which help Bezos' motivation to continue growing Amazon into the best e-commerce store on the market.

A Ralph Waldo Emerson Quote

Like most people, one of the ways Bezos keeps in contact with his customers is through social media platforms. It was through his Twitter profile that people found one of the ways Bezos stays motivated. In a post, he shared a quote by Ralph Waldo Emerson, which states "To laugh often and much; to win the respect of intelligent people and affection of children; to earn the appreciation of honest critics and endure betrayal of false friends; to appreciate beauty; to find the best in others; to leave the world a bit better, whether by a healthy child, a garden patch, or redeemed social condition; to know even one life has breathed easier because you have lived. This is to have succeeded."[17] Every morning, Bezos reads this

---

[17] Savona, 2018.

quote, which hangs on his fridge. He uses it as a source of motivation for the day as it helps him remember what success is truly about.

It's Okay to Be Terrified

Not all of Bezos' motivational advice has been favored by his critics and his customers. In fact, when people read that one of the pieces of advice Bezos gave his employees, which was to wake up terrified, people were shocked. They could not understand why someone who prides himself of leading a great team would give his employees such distasteful advice. Why would he want them to wake up terrified?

Bezos explained that he feels fear brings out motivation. Therefore, as Bezos spoke to his employees about waking up terrified, he was trying to get them to feel motivated about their position at Amazon. He wants his employees to take on this mindset because it will make them think about the future. Bezos stated that everyone knows they work for one of the biggest e-commerce companies. However, they have to remember that this might not be true in the future, which means they should be terrified about this prospect. If they are afraid, they will stay motivated to stay on top of their work and help keep the company on top.

Bezos stated that if his team fears customer complaints, they will work harder to make sure every customer is happy with the service. If his staff fear that one of Amazon's new products won't work correctly, they will become motivated to develop the best product possible. At the same time, Bezos realizes that this is a bit of a fine line because people can refuse to try new ideas because of fear. Therefore, he also advocates that even if a service fails, it doesn't mean that the company fails. Instead, they pick up the pieces and carry them on into the future. After all, Amazon has already shown that they can take a device which fails and turn it into something better and successful.

Find Your Calling, Not Your Career

Jeff Bezos often tells people that knowing he has found his calling is one of his biggest motivators. He doesn't feel like he has a job or a career, he feels like he has found what he was truly meant to do with his life. Because he sees businesses as callings, he doesn't feel like it's work, which makes it easier to accomplish everything he needs to do. Instead, he found something that gives him substance in his life. In other words, the responsibilities he has are the juice that keeps him going throughout the day. It makes him want to get up the next morning and repeat everything over again. It makes him want to go into his office, read the customer emails, and continue to work with his team on new products. The more passionate you are about what you want to accomplish, the more motivated you will feel.

Focus on Your Passion, Not Anyone Else's Passion

I just discussed how Bezos believes you need to find what you're passionate about in order to remain motivated. With this, it's also important to remember that you have to find what you are passionate about and not what everyone else is. Think of when Bezos first started Amazon out of his garage. It was a bookstore meant for the internet, which was a new feature in the world. Therefore, Bezos was not doing something that he felt everyone was passionate about. He was doing something he felt passionate about. He felt passionate about establishing an e-commerce store which would begin by selling books but also sell other products over time. He also felt passionate about how the internet was the future of the world. Through these passions, Bezos was able to create the Amazon empire.

Start Small but Go Big

I have already discussed how Amazon started small. Bezos always had the idea of expanding Amazon beyond a bookstore, but he also knew that he had to start small and then go big. He also credits this mindset as one of his motivations. Because he had this bigger picture for Amazon, he wanted to make sure he accomplished that picture. While Amazon was still a bookstore, he felt motivated to do well so he could incorporate CDs and DVDs into the store. From there, he became motivated to work towards adding clothing and then jewelry. With each new addition for Amazon, Bezos found the motivation to continue when he thought of the next product or service he could add.

Don't Take Criticism Too Personally

From the beginning, Bezos and Amazon have been no strangers to critics. People didn't believe that Amazon would make it as an e-commerce store. This didn't stop Bezos from continuing on his dream of establishing one of the biggest e-commerce stores in this generation. In fact, when Bezos talks to other people about critics, he often jokes by stating "If you absolutely cannot tolerate critics, don't do anything new or interesting."[18] What Bezos means by this is that not everyone is going to like what you are doing. This doesn't make it a bad idea or service. In fact, the best products in the world have received some of the harshest criticism. Therefore, you never want to believe what every critic states and you never want to take it personally.

This doesn't mean that you should ignore criticism. Similar to listening to negative customer feedback, you can grow your business through the criticism. It is similar to turning a negative into a positive. You can take what is said, think

---

[18] Bourne, 2018.

critically about it, and then see if there is anything that you can improve on. If there is, then you can go ahead and improve the product. However, if there isn't then you move forward and leave the criticism there.

Be Happy

Previously, I talked about how Bezos doesn't believe in the professional and personal life balance; he believes that you need to integrate the two and create a circle. This belief ties into another factor which motivates him and this is simply to be happy. Bezos states when he is happy with his life at home, he is a good father and when he happy with his life at work, he is a good supervisor and CEO. Bezos knows that happiness brings many benefits not only into his life but the lives of those around him.

Bezos believes that when you are happy, you will be able to think more clearly, you will remain more flexible, and you will strive to do your best every day. These are important pieces of motivation. People are more energized to complete their responsibilities when they feel positive. They not only feel that they can do the work well, but they will also be proud of their accomplishment. This will lead them to feel motivated to do more. However, if people feel negatively about a task, they feel that they won't be able to perform the work well. This means that they will be less likely to feel motivated to complete their responsibilities.

There is No Difference between You and the Person at the Top

Another factor that Bezos states is a good motivator is realizing that anyone can sit where he sits. He wants people to remember that at one time, he was just like everyone else. He struggled to pay the bills and Amazon wasn't always the biggest e-commerce store on the market. He wants people to realize that there is no difference between them and the CEO of any company. Just as many CEOs built their company from scratch, you can do the same thing.

Your Choices are Part of Your Story

Bezos often discusses how no matter who you are, you will leave a story. This story is made up of all the decisions that you made throughout your life. Therefore, you will want to do everything you can to make sure you are making the best decisions so you can leave the greatest story. Furthermore, if you work towards making your best choices, you will feel motivated on your journey.

Bezos also states that you don't have to always make a decision immediately. Sometimes you will be able to map out decisions in your mind prior to needing an answer while other times you will be able to think about your choice. By doing this, you will be able to reinforce the foundation that makes your story great. In return, you will feel motivated to continue on your path.

Don't Let Your Failures Get the Best of You

Bezos is open about how he has spent close to billions of dollars in failures at Amazon. He also tells people while some failures can be harder than others, he never lets the failures get to him. He also advises his employees not to focus on the failures. Instead, they are supposed to learn from their failures and focus on their successes. After all, Amazon has spent more money on all their successful business ventures than their failures. As Bezos believes, even if you have hundreds of failures and a few major successes, the successes outweigh the failures.

Focus on Your Company's Mission

Every company needs a vision and a mission. For Amazon, the mission and vision is "to be earth's most customer-centric company; to build a place where people can come to find and discover anything they might want to buy online."[19] Bezos believes that one of the biggest things that can motivate a person to do well in their company is by sticking to their mission.

Bezos has seen many CEOs and other supervisors in a company turn their back on the mission. In response, the

---

[19] Bourne, 2018.

company started to take a turn for the worst. Not only did loyal customers stop shopping at these companies, but some of the companies went bankrupt. Bezos states that forgetting about the reason you established the company is the first grave mistake you can make. As long as you keep your vision and mission in mind, you will be able to stay motivated and make sure every employee follows the mission.

Remember That People Count on You

Bezos has stated that another one of his biggest motivational factors is that he knows people count on him. Not only does his Amazon team count on him but his customers, followers, inspiring entrepreneurs, and his family do as well. Because of this, Bezos stays motivated to make sure he is always doing the best job he can. He wants to make sure that he is making the right decisions for his customers and his team. He wants to make sure that he is not only giving advice to young entrepreneurs but that he is also following his own advice. All these pieces motivate Bezos to continue to work towards the mission of Amazon, work towards space colonization, and make the best decisions so he can leave a great story.

Think About What You Really Want

A few years ago, a shareholder letter came out which explained to people an interesting offer that Jeff Bezos gives to his Amazon employees. This offer starts by Bezos sending an email to his employees asking them not to take the following offer, which pays them a few thousand dollars plus one month's salary to quit their job.

Of course, Bezos doesn't really want any member of his team to take the offer. However, he also only wants people who truly want to work at Amazon. He wants people who are motivated to do their best for the company. He states that by sending out this offer, which he will pay if someone leaves, he is able to weed out the people who truly want to see Amazon succeed and the people who consider Amazon to be just another paycheck.

This is a reverse psychological tactic that Bezos uses in order to make his staff think about what they really want to gain from their job. If they only care about the money, they are most likely going to take the offer and move on to their next job. However, if they are motivated to do their best and help bring the company into the future then they will choose to stay with Amazon and decline the offer.

Chapter 13: Advice from Jeff Bezos

Not only is Jeff Bezos one of the greatest businessmen in modern history, but he is also known to give people a wide range of advice. While I have already discussed a lot of Bezos' business beliefs and strategies, he also realizes that the CEO and higher ups of a company can help make a company successful or cause a company to fail. Therefore, throughout his presentation, Bezos is known to not only give business advice but also life advice. In fact, because of this, many people have started to see the Amazon CEO as more of a person than a billionaire behind a trillion dollar company.

The advice that Bezos gives comes to him the same way as his business advice, which is through his experiences in life. Bezos strongly believes that people can learn from his mistakes and life stories. In fact, some people believe that one of the best ways you can get to know Jeff Bezos as a person is through the advice and help he gives to other people.

Don't Have Regrets

While it is often human nature to feel some regret about our mistakes, Bezos believes that this can be a bigger problem than the failure itself. Regrets can often hold us back, which means that we won't take the risks that Bezos often tells us we should be taking. Regretting can bring out fear in a person, which can make them anxious about making a certain decision. Even if this idea could succeed, even if all the measurements point to the idea as being a great one, if you regret past mistakes you will be afraid to take the idea further.

Schedule Meetings Early in the Day

Even though Bezos made sure he was home to have breakfast in the morning with his family, he also made sure to schedule his most thought-provoking meetings once he got to work. Bezos states that just because he has a great amount of energy, gets a full night's sleep, and is overall incredibly happy in his life doesn't mean he doesn't feel tired or sluggish near the end of the day. Just like everyone else Bezos tends to feel a lack of energy near the end of the workday. This is why he tends to schedule his most high-quality meetings around 10:00 in the morning.

On top of this, he won't focus on certain things when he doesn't have the energy. For example, if it is 5:00 in the afternoon and Bezos receives a question that he feels he can't rightfully answer at that time, he will schedule the meeting for right away in the morning. He doesn't force himself to come up with an answer because he feels he doesn't have the right energy or brain power to put towards that decision now. And because making a decision because he was asked the question at the end of the day could harm his company more than help it, he feels it's best to wait until he is fully rested.

Find Your Own Way

Many entrepreneurs tend to look to see what other companies are doing before they start up their business. Bezos states that this is not the correct way to go about starting up for two main reasons. First, you won't be passionate about what you are doing. When you are following the crowd, you are doing what everyone else is doing. Doing this can easily make you lose interest in the work, which can have negative effects on your company.

Second, you won't have a unique company. Bezos believes that one of the reasons Amazon has stayed on top for so long is because it's a company that wasn't like any other company at the time. Yes, it started out as a bookstore, but Bezos always had plans to take the company farther. On top of that, he did make his online bookstore different from the rest because it had a larger variety of books, specifically the rare books that other people couldn't find. Furthermore, he created an online bookstore that allowed credit cards, this was something that was brand new in the online market. Therefore, while Bezos took a common store idea, he found his own way to do it.

When it comes to people asking Bezos what his best advice is for new and young entrepreneurs, this is the piece he talks about. He believes that finding your own way by focusing on something you're passionate about and making sure it is different from what everyone else is doing is number one. He tells people that they should position themselves in a location where they work hard, continue to follow their dreams, but also watch the wave of their success come at them.

Even if you feel that your passionate idea might not take off, go for it anyway. Remember, Bezos did not think that Amazon would be successful when he first started the company in 1995. In fact, he felt the company could still fail into the early 2000s. However, Bezos kept his passions in mind and continue to work towards building his business his way.

Be Proud of Your Choices, Not Your Talents

Another piece of advice Bezos shares with not only entrepreneurs but also children is that they should be more proud of their choices than their talents. He states that everyone has talents and they are a great thing to have and be proud of, especially if your talents are helpful for yourself and other people. But, he also believes that people should be more proud of the decisions they make because it is these choices that will lead them to become successful.

Bezos states that when you apply yourself to make the best choices, you will be able to take your talents further than you ever imagined. Therefore, it's not your talents that you should focus on, but the decisions you make which surround your talents. Your self-worth should come from your results and not because you're good at math or you're a good singer.

Keep Your Childlike Sense of Wonder

Bezos states that many entrepreneurs fall into the role of losing their childlike sense of wonder. What this means is that they don't follow their true passions. Instead, they let their intellectual side take over, which is often the side of us which makes us lose our passions. Therefore, Bezos states that you always want to keep that childlike side in you as it will help you remain passionate, which will help you succeed in the business world. On top of remaining passionate about what you doing, you will also feel happier overall. When discussing this in his speeches, Bezos asks people to take a moment to think about their childhood or children in general. Think about how happy they are and how they strive to do what they want to do. That is the piece you need to keep as an entrepreneur.

Go to Bed

Bezos is very honest about his daily schedule, and a big part of this schedule is going to be so he can get a good amount of sleep every night. It takes a lot of energy to run a successful business and still be there for your family. As I discussed earlier in this book, Bezos found a way to do this, however, he would have never been able to accomplish his schedule without getting enough sleep.

Bezos points out that entrepreneurs are not around to make thousands of decisions every day; they are around to make the most high-quality decisions they can. This takes a lot of critical thinking, which can take a lot of energy. Therefore, Bezos states that you need at least a full eight hours of sleep every night. No matter how busy your schedule is, you need to make sure to block out enough hours at night so you can sleep well. Otherwise, you will start to feel sluggish, have low energy, and soon you will find your company fading along with you.

For Your Competitors, Be Their Role Model

I've already mentioned in this book that Bezos doesn't keep up with his competitors. He doesn't care how they run their business and he doesn't pay attention to how well his competitors are doing. One of the reasons for this is because he believes that he should be a role model for his competitors. He believes, and has stated during several occasions, that other businesses should use the policies he set up for Amazon. Bezos sees himself as a role model for his competitors because his business is doing great, he continues to remain at the top, and his policies have been proven to work when building up a gigantic company.

Always Keep Your Health in Mind

Bezos fully understands how busy lives can be. He fully understands how hard it can be to find a way to link your professional and personal life together. However, he also knows how important keeping your health at the front of the line is. People often feel that they can't go to the doctor because they have meetings all day or they feel that they can't take a break because they have so much work to do. Bezos believes this is one of the worst things you can do to yourself.

Bezos wants you to think of it this way – if you are not taking care of yourself, how can you take care of your company and your family? You have to feel great yourself in order to make sure your company and your family are well taken care of. Even if this means that you take time away from your company. You don't have to be there every day for every single thing. This is why you hire managers that you can trust to take care of your company while you are away.

Bezos also believes that things can wait. You can wait to make decisions until you are fully capable of making them. You can wait to hire someone until you are able to find the best person not only for that specific job but for the company as a whole. He doesn't ever want entrepreneurs to feel they are forced to make decisions in their company immediately. After all,

Bezos states it is your company and this is something that you should never forget.

Don't Stop Thinking Ahead

Amazon is known for usually being one step ahead of everyone else. This is because one of Bezos' policies for himself and his team is to always think ahead. As Bezos stated himself, "All of our senior executives operate the same way I do. They work in the future, they live in the future."[20] Not only does he state you should think days, weeks, and months ahead but you should also think years ahead. Bezos always welcomes ideas from his employees, and he is known to do one of these things when he hears an idea from his staff.

1. He will think of certain questions about the idea. There are times when Bezos has done this that many members of his staff feel he was being highly critical of their decision. In fact, some employees have felt belittled by Bezos. However, Bezos doesn't see it as being highly critical or belittling, he sees it as making sure everything has been thought of when it comes to this idea. It's the same process he does to himself when he comes up with an idea. He looks into everything he

---

[20] Barrabi, 2018.

can before taking the idea into further consideration.

2. He will ask his employee what this idea will to do for the company in the future. He doesn't ask them to just think of month in advance but years, as far as they can take the idea. Will the idea be useful for Amazon in 10 years or 15 years?

3. Can this idea lead to something bigger? Bezos is a person who knows that a small idea can turn into something huge. After all, he built Amazon from scratch. Another example is the Kindle e-Reader. This device started as a black and white tablet so people could hold several books and bring them everywhere they went and grew into the Kindle Fire, which allows you to do anything that an iPad allows you to do. In fact, when the Kindle Fire was first released around the same time as the Apple iPad 2, people wondered if the Kindle Fire would end the iPad.

4. If he finds the idea to be a great idea, he will take the next steps to make the idea into a device with his staff. They will not only measure the idea to make sure it's feasible to try but measure everything beyond the idea they do.

Success is not going to Happen Overnight

Another large piece of advice that Bezos gives new entrepreneurs is that your success is not going to happen overnight. Even though Amazon did well in its first month in 1995, the company didn't hit mainstream success until into the early 2000s. Bezos wants people to remember not to get frustrated when their company is first starting up. In fact, he doesn't want the CEOs to become frustrated, or worse, think of giving up within the company's first few years. Bezos feels it's very important that you know success is not going to happen anywhere near overnight. In fact, Bezos often tells people that it takes about a decade to become an overnight success.

Being misunderstood is Being Innovative

Bezos feels that sometimes entrepreneurs will only do certain things or won't do some things because they feel that if they are misunderstood they will never make it. However, Bezos feels the opposite way. He states that the more you are willing to be misunderstood, the more your company will grow. Not everyone is going to understand your ideas or your new products, but this doesn't mean that they won't become one of the best pieces of merchandise in your company. Even if it takes time for people to catch on to the usefulness of your new creation, it can still become successful in the future. This is why you always want to think far into the future when you're being innovative, even if you are misunderstood at the time.

Chapter 14: A Future Outlook

While it is nearly impossible to tell the future, it is easy to see how the future outlook for Amazon is very impressive. As Bezos often discusses in his presentations, he is going to do whatever he can to make sure Amazon reaches 100% customer satisfaction. Through reading this biography, you know that Bezos has focused on what his customers wanted from day one and he never plans to steer his company away from their customer service satisfaction policies. After all, the company is always running on a day one policy.

There are many newer areas that Amazon is focusing on, such as artificial intelligence, their drone experiment, and many other services and products that anyone outside of Amazon's headquarters has yet to hear about. Therefore, when it comes to the future of Amazon, you should know that some of it will focus on artificial intelligence, drones, other forms of technology as this is one of Bezos' main advancement areas, and robots. In fact, robots are already working in places within Amazon. They have started to alleviate some of the pressure and stress of several employees by being able to do some of the tasks they were accomplishing. Of course, this doesn't mean that the employees have less to do. Instead, it means that the employees are able to focus on other details to help bring Amazon into the future.

But, just what is the drone experiment? This is something that Amazon has been working on for at least a couple of years. The goal is to develop dozens of drones which will be able to bring a customer's order to them within 30 minutes. While the public testing that Amazon has done with the drone delivery service has failed, this doesn't mean that they decided to place the drones on a shelf. Instead, it means that they will go back to the creative table and find something which allows them to improve the drone's performance. Bezos knows that while many Amazon customers love Amazon Prime, people don't like to wait. He knows that when customers purchase an item, they want it as quickly as possible. Therefore, Bezos and his creative team have been working towards trying to figure out the best way to do this. After all, this will lead to a higher customer satisfaction rating for the company.

Then, there are people who are paying attention to what has become known as the India Experiment. Over the last few years, Amazon has been growing in India, launching Amazon Prime and spending a lot of money on plans to broaden its services in the country. While this only led most of Amazon's critics to state that the company is trying to take over the world, Amazon continued to go forward with their plans to reach out to people living in India. With future plans unveiled by Bezos, there is still much more to come for those living in India and probably other countries around the world.

The way Amazon is delivering groceries will also see changes in the future. For example, the company might be coming out with a smart fridge, which is often referred to as an Echo Fridge. This is a fridge that has a specific design, a screen where you could reorder Amazon food items from, and an Alexa enabled voice.

You might be someone who can't imagine Amazon getting any bigger than it already is or you might be someone who can imagine Amazon taking over the world. Whatever you imagine, the future of Amazon looks promising and that, as Bezos believes, will continue to grow in the right direction as long as the Amazon team continues to follow customer satisfaction and stay one step ahead in providing their customers with what they need.

Conclusion

There are many inspirational people in the world and Jeff Bezos is definitely one of them. Even if you don't want to own your own business, there is still a lot of life and career advice that you can take into consideration through Bezos' life work. For example, no matter where you work, if you are in a supervisor position listening to your staff is a great quality to have. You can take other advice from this book, or advice that you continue to find in your research about Bezos and incorporate it into your life. Not only has Jeff Bezos become the richest man in the world, but he has also become a person who is willing to share helpful advice for your professional journey.

This book not only brought you into the early years of one of the most successful businessmen of the modern era, but it also brought you on his professional journey. It focused on Bezos' many business lessons that he often shares with his audience while he is speaking in a public setting. This book also brought you into the mind of Jeff Bezos so you could get a better sense of how he became a business titan. It showed you what Bezos says motivates him, what advice he often gives not only to entrepreneurs but also to children and any young adult, and what possibilities the future holds for Amazon.

Above all, this biography on the first few decades of Jeff

Bezos' life focused on his last 30 years – his career. Specifically, this book focused on the business side of Bezos. Hopefully, you found this biography to be especially helpful if you are looking at starting your own business or at the beginning of your professional career. However, this book can also help you if you have been running your own business for a few years. Like Bezos believes, it is always a great idea to look into other businesses, no matter how long your business has been established. This can not only help you take your business a step further in the right direction, but it can also help you go a step further in becoming the best business owner that you can be.

This is one of the biggest pieces of advice that Bezos brings to the world. You want to constantly evolve into something better. You want to continue to grow your company so it can become the best company possible. On top of that, you want to continue to raise the bar not only with your employees but also with yourself as this will help your company grow in the most positive way, just as Amazon has for Bezos and his team.

Some of the biggest factors to take away from this business biography are the helpful policies and guidelines that Bezos has been using since he first established Amazon. One of these is you always want to make sure that your customers are number one. By now, Bezos and his team have proven with Amazon that the more you focus on customer satisfaction, the more you will get out of your business. Another factor is to take risks. Even though you might find that your risk wasn't financially helpful for your company in the short-term, Bezos always wants you to look into the long-term. Remember, if your risk helps your company long-term, then you should continue that product or service. Always remember to collect your data. Amazon loves to collect data and even Jeff Bezos admits that they tend to collect data over things he initially thought were silly. However, this data has also proven to help the company on more than one occasion.

Furthermore, you never want to give up. As long as you put in your best effort, you have been successful. Not everything is going to work out in your favor and you will make mistakes on your professional journey. The best thing to do when this happens, as Bezos believes, is to learn from these mistakes. It's possible that while your product didn't work out the first time, you can reinvent your product so it is bigger and better for the future.

This brings me to another point that Bezos often stresses and that is to always look towards the future. Look at your past so you can continue to learn from your mistakes and then look towards the future so you can do something better. Bezos wants you to remember to look into the future as this will help you stay one step ahead of not only your competition but your customers. By looking towards the future, you will be able to learn what your customers want that they don't even know they want. This is a philosophy that not only Bezos follows but also other CEOs such as Steve Jobs followed. As Bezos states, people don't often know what they want until they have it right in front of them.

Today, when Bezos looks back at his business journey, he realizes that it was the leadership he practiced with Amazon, the company's policies, and the way they conduct their business that led to his success. It was also the fact that the company has never been hesitant to take risks. This is why Bezos travels and speaks about the way he conducts his business. He doesn't tell entrepreneurs to conduct business his way because he is arrogant. He tells entrepreneurs to handle business the way he has because it works. Bezos, who does not worry about his competition, wants people to become successful in their careers.

This book has brought you to the end of Jeff Bezos' journey, as of now. Remember, Bezos is only in his mid-50s and he still has several years ahead of him. Not only is Amazon still one of the most successful e-commerce businesses in the United States, but the company continues to grow all over the world. On top of this, Bezos has only started his business within Blue Origin. He is a man who is constantly thinking of what steps he can take next in his life. In reality, you never know what you will read about next when it comes to Jeff Bezos.

Bibliography

4 Business Thoughts from Jeff Bezos for Young Entrepreneurs. (2018). Retrieved from https://medium.com/swlh/4-business-thoughts-from-jeff-bezos-for-young-entrepreneurs-f021315221d.

Abbott, R. (2018). 'It's Always Day 1 at Amazon:' The Bezos Philosophy, Part 10 - GuruFocus.com. Retrieved from https://www.gurufocus.com/news/684616/its-always-day-1-at-amazon-the-bezos-philosophy-part-10.

Alton, L. (2016). 5 Things Every Entrepreneur Should Know About Risk-Taking. Retrieved from https://www.entrepreneur.com/article/270320.

Amazon.com: Customer reviews: Turning on bright minds: A parent looks at gifted education in Texas. (2013). Retrieved from https://www.amazon.com/Turning-bright-minds-parent-education/product-reviews/B0006CTR1A.

Amazon's global career site. Retrieved from https://www.amazon.jobs/en/principles.

Barrabi, T. (2018). Jeff Bezos' 5 tips for running a successful business. Retrieved from https://www.foxbusiness.com/business-leaders/jeff-bezos-5-tips-for-running-a-successful-business.

Baldacci, K. (2013). 7 Customer Service Lessons from Amazon CEO Jeff Bezos. Retrieved from https://www.salesforce.com/blog/2013/06/jeff-bezos-lessons.html.

Bernard, Z. (2019). Jeff Bezos' advice to Amazon employees is to stop aiming for work-life 'balance' — here's what you should strive for instead. Retrieved from https://www.businessinsider.com/jeff-bezo-advice-to-amazon-employees-dont-aim-for-work-life-balance-its-a-circle-2018-4.

The Bezos Day One Fund. Retrieved from https://www.bezosdayonefund.org/.

Bezos, J. (2017). 2016 Letter to Shareholders. Retrieved from https://ir.aboutamazon.com/static-files/e01cc6e7-73df-4860-bd3d-95d366f29e57.

Bourne, Z. (2019). What Motivates the World's Richest Man, Jeff Bezos?. Retrieved from https://addicted2success.com/entrepreneur-profile/what-motivates-the-worlds-richest-man-jeff-bezos/.

Brandt, R. (2011). One Click: Jeff Bezos and the Rise of Amazon.com. Kindle Edition.

Carlson, N. (2011). Jeff Bezos: Here's Why He Won. Retrieved from https://www.businessinsider.com/jeff-bezos-visionary-2011-4.

Daskal, L. 10 Simple Ways You Can Stop Yourself From Overthinking. Retrieved from https://www.inc.com/lolly-daskal/10-simple-ways-you-can-stop-yourself-from-overthinking.html.

Feloni, R. (2015). Jeff Bezos shares his best advice to entrepreneurs. Retrieved from https://www.businessinsider.com/jeff-bezos-best-advice-to-entrepreneurs-2015-2.

Gilbert, B. (2019). Jeff Bezos explains how creating the Echo was a huge risk for Amazon that was worth taking. Retrieved from https://www.businessinsider.com/jeff-bezos-says-echo-was-huge-risk-for-amazon-worth-taking-2019-4.

Greathouse, J. (2004). Ten Startup Tips From Amazon Founder, Jeff Bezos | John Greathouse. Retrieved from http://johngreathouse.com/10tips-bezos/.

Green, D. (2018). Amazon's struggles with its Fresh grocery service show a huge liability for Prime. Retrieved from https://www.businessinsider.com/amazon-fresh-struggles-show-a-huge-liability-in-prime-2018-7.

Hartmans, A., & Akhtar, A. (2019). Jeff Bezos Finalized His Divorce Agreement for 75% of Amazon Stock. Here's How He Built the $1 Trillion Company to Become the World's

Richest Man. Retrieved from
https://www.businessinsider.com/amazon-ceo-jeff-bezos-richest-man-world-career-life-story-2017-7.

Hoffower, H. (2019). We did the math to calculate how much money Jeff Bezos makes in a year, month, week, day, hour, minute, and second. Retrieved from
https://www.businessinsider.com/what-amazon-ceo-jeff-bezos-makes-every-day-hour-minute-2018-10.

Jeff Bezos Uses This Strategy to Make Better, Faster Decisions. (2018). Retrieved from
https://www.inc.com/quora/jeff-bezos-uses-this-strategy-to-make-better-faster-decisions.html.

Kim, E. (2019). Jeff Bezos used to hate spending money on ads, but told employees in November he 'changed his mind'. Retrieved from https://www.cnbc.com/2019/02/02/jeff-bezos-says-hes-had-a-change-of-heart-on-advertising--now-amazon-is-the-fifth-biggest-ad-spender-in-the-us-.html.

Maharishi, A. (2019). Sagacious Business Nuggets From Jeff Bezos. Retrieved from
https://www.entrepreneur.com/article/331942.

McGolerick, E. (2017). What Is Montessori Preschool? Finally, Montessori Explained. Retrieved from
https://www.sheknows.com/parenting/articles/1006195/what-is-a-montessori-preschool/.

Medeiros, J. (2018). 6 Powerful Things Jeff Bezos Wants You To Know About Success. Retrieved from https://www.goalcast.com/2018/04/04/what-jeff-bezos-wants-you-to-know-about-success/.

Mejia, Z. (2018). Amazon CEO Jeff Bezos shares the career advice he gives his kids. Retrieved from https://www.cnbc.com/2018/11/15/amazon-ceo-jeff-bezos-shares-the-career-advice-he-gives-his-kids.html.

Montag, A. (2018). This is Jeff Bezos' 3-question test for new Amazon employees. Retrieved from https://www.cnbc.com/2018/08/01/jeff-bezos-questions-amazon-used-to-hire-employees.html.

Morris, J. (2017) Jeff Bezos: Think like Jeff Bezos - Making of an e-commerce business mammoth from yesterday for tomorrow: 23 life-changing lessons from Jeff Bezos on Life, People, Business, Technology and Leadership. Kindle Edition.

Murayama, K. (2018). The science of motivation. Retrieved from https://www.apa.org/science/about/psa/2018/06/motivation.

Patel, N. (2019). 12 Business Lessons You Can Learn from Amazon Founder and CEO Jeff Bezos. Retrieved from https://neilpatel.com/blog/lessons-from-jeff-bezos/.

Premack, R. (2018). Jeff Bezos said the 'secret sauce' to Amazon's success is an 'obsessive compulsive focus' on customer over competitor. Retrieved from https://www.businessinsider.com/amazon-jeff-bezos-success-customer-obsession-2018-9.

Prest, M. (2019). Former Amazon VP Will Lead Jeff Bezos's Day One Academies Fund. Retrieved from https://www.philanthropy.com/article/Former-Amazon-VP-Will-Lead/245409.

Rodgers, T. Bezos Launches Day One Fund. Retrieved from https://www.whiteboardadvisors.com/article/bezos-launches-day-one-fund-0.

Savona, B. (2018). Here are the words Jeff Bezos relies on for motivation every morning. Retrieved from https://www.smartcompany.com.au/business-advice/quote-amazon-ceo-jeff-bezos-read-every-morning/.

Seltzer, L. (2017). Yes, You Can't!—Why You Should Affirm Your Limitations. Retrieved from https://www.psychologytoday.com/us/blog/evolution-the-self/201707/yes-you-can-t-why-you-should-affirm-your-limitations.

Shaban, H. (2018). Amazon is issued patent for delivery drones that can react to screaming voices, flailing arms. Retrieved from https://www.washingtonpost.com/news/the-switch/wp/2018/03/22/amazon-issued-patent-for-delivery-drones-that-can-react-to-screaming-flailing-arms/?utm_term=.44ceba87981a.

Sullivan, S. (2013). The politics of Jeff Bezos. Retrieved from https://www.washingtonpost.com/news/the-fix/wp/2013/08/07/the-politics-of-jeff-bezos/?utm_term=.a3070efe1fcd.

The Bezos Day One Fund. Retrieved from https://www.bezosdayonefund.org/.

Tsagklis, I. (2018). 8 Inspiring Jeff Bezos Quotes on Business and Success. Retrieved from https://medium.com/@iliastsagklis/8-inspiring-jeff-bezos-quotes-on-business-and-success-d22059e51445.

Wald, E. (2018). Saudi crown prince woos Amazon, Lockheed and others to build a tech hub. Retrieved from https://www.cnbc.com/2018/04/13/saudi-crown-prince-woos-amazon-lockheed-and-others-to-build-a-tech-hub.html.

Wulfhart, N. 7 Signs You're Overthinking That Big Decision. Retrieved from https://www.themuse.com/advice/7-signs-youre-overthinking-that-big-decision.